How to Use This Book

Look for these special features in this book:

SIDEBARS, **CHARTS**, **GRAPHS**, and original **MAPS** expand your understanding of what's being discussed—and also make useful sources for classroom reports.

FAQs answer common **F**requently **A**sked **Q**uestions about people, places, and things.

WOW FACTORS offer "Who knew?" facts to keep you thinking.

TRAVEL GUIDE gives you tips on exploring the state—either in person or right from your chair!

PROJECT ROOM provides fun ideas for school assignments and incredible research projects. Plus, there's a guide to primary sources—what they are and how to cite them.

Please note: All statistics are as up-to-date as possible at the time of publication.

Consultants: William Loren Katz; Philip J. Roberts, Professor of History, University of Wyoming; Erin Campbell-Stone, Department of Geology and Geophysics, University of Wyoming

Book production by The Design Lab

Library of Congress Cataloging-in-Publication Data
Prentzas, G. S.
 Wyoming / by G.S. Prentzas.
    p. cm.—(America the beautiful. Third series)
Includes bibliographical references and index.
ISBN-13: 978-0-531-18508-7
ISBN-10: 0-531-18508-7
1. Wyoming—Juvenile literature. I. Title. II. Series.
F761.3.P74 2008
978.7—dc22   2008016789

1 2 3 4 5 6 7 8 9 10 R 19 18 17 16 15 14 13 12 11 10

AMERICA ★ THE ★ BEAUTIFUL

Wyoming

BY G. S. PRENTZAS

Third Series

Children's Press®
An Imprint of Scholastic Inc.
New York ★ Toronto ★ London ★ Auckland ★ Sydney
Mexico City ★ New Delhi ★ Hong Kong
Danbury, Connecticut

CONTENTS

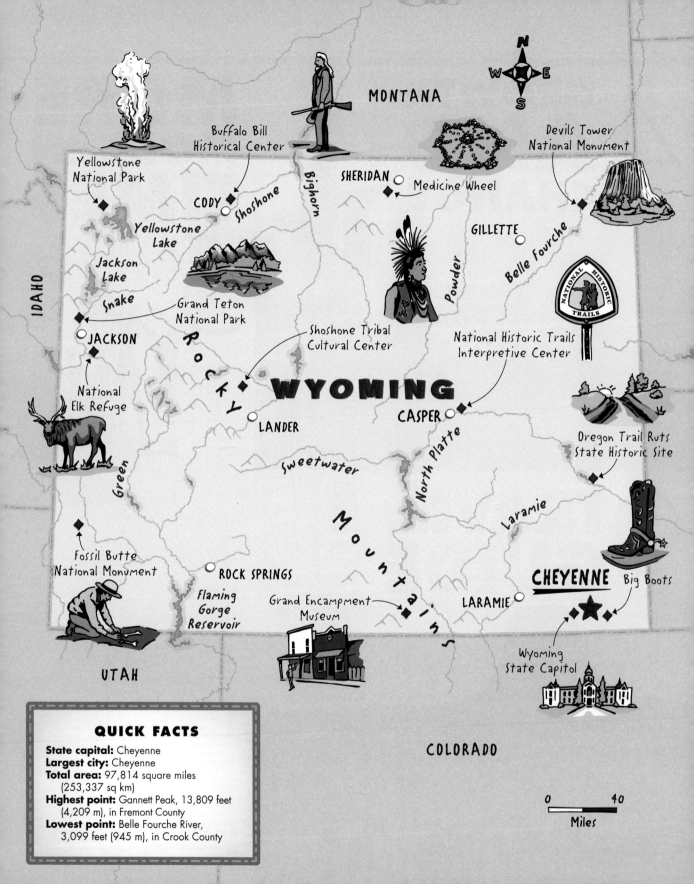

MONTANA

Buffalo Bill
Historical Center

Yellowstone
National Park

Devils Tower
National Monument

Medicine Wheel

SHERIDAN

CODY   Shoshone

Bighorn

GILLETTE

Belle Fourche

Yellowstone
Lake

Powder

NATIONAL HISTORIC
TRAILS

Jackson
Lake

IDAHO

Snake

Grand Teton
National Park

Shoshone Tribal
Cultural Center

National Historic Trails
Interpretive Center

WYOMING

JACKSON

ROCKY

CASPER

National
Elk Refuge

LANDER

Oregon Trail Ruts
State Historic Site

Sweetwater

North Platte

Green

Laramie

Fossil Butte
National Monument

ROCK SPRINGS

Mountains

CHEYENNE   Big Boots

Flaming
Gorge
Reservoir

Grand Encampment
Museum

LARAMIE

UTAH

Wyoming
State Capitol

COLORADO

QUICK FACTS

State capital: Cheyenne
Largest city: Cheyenne
Total area: 97,814 square miles
(253,337 sq km)
Highest point: Gannett Peak, 13,809 feet
(4,209 m), in Fremont County
Lowest point: Belle Fourche River,
3,099 feet (945 m), in Crook County

0   40
Miles

SOUTH
DAKOTA

MINNESOTA

NEBRASKA

IOWA

KANSAS

Welcome to Wyoming!

HOW DID WYOMING GET ITS NAME?

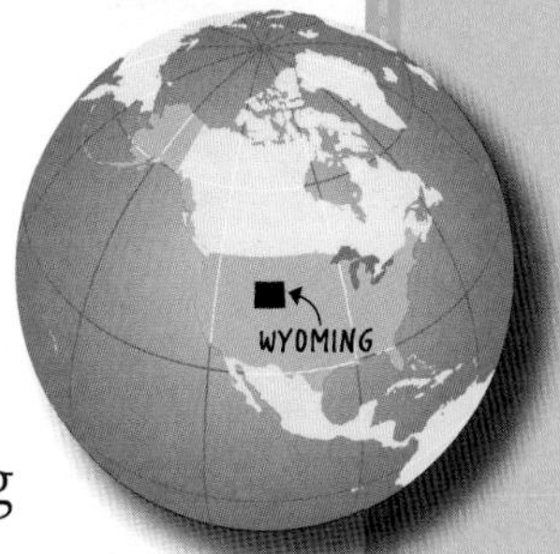

The name *Wyoming* comes from two words in the language of the Delaware people: *wama,* meaning "plains," and *maughwau,* meaning "large." In 1869, the Wyoming Territory was organized from three existing western territories that covered huge areas of flat land: Dakota, Idaho, and Utah. Congress called the territory Wyoming because that name had been commonly used for the region.

WYOMING

8

READ ABOUT

A view of the
Teton Range from
Schwabacher
Landing in
Grand Teton
National Park

LAND

★

W YOMING IS ALMOST A PERFECT RECTANGLE—ABOUT 276 MILES (444 KILOMETERS) NORTH TO SOUTH AND 375 MILES (604 KM) EAST TO WEST. However, its natural beauty is anything but neat and square. Across its 97,814 square miles (253,337 sq km), the state boasts high mountains and multicolored canyons, wide-open deserts and quiet plains. Its lowest point—at the Belle Fourche River in Crook County—lies at 3,099 feet (945 meters) above sea level. Its highest point, Gannett Peak, soars to 13,809 feet (4,209 m).

Scientists dig at Como Bluff, searching for dinosaur bones.

WORDS TO KNOW

geologists *scientists who study the history of Earth*

receded *pulled or moved back over time*

ROCK AND WATER

Geologists believe that the oldest rocks in Wyoming are more than 3 billion years old. Since that time, many different natural forces have shaped Wyoming's landscape.

Wyoming is halfway between the Mississippi River and the Pacific Ocean. But from about 600 million to 300 million years ago, a sea covered much of North America, including Wyoming. The sea **receded** and advanced again and again, leaving behind a new layer of sand, clay, and salt each time. The layers compacted under their own weight and became rock. In parts of the state, geologists have found the remains of crocodile-like reptiles and primitive fishes in this rock.

Around 300 million years ago, huge chunks of Earth's crust pushed against each other, causing the seafloor in Wyoming to buckle upward, forming underwater mountains. Once the seawater receded, **erosion** ate away mountain peaks. Snowmelt, rainwater, and wind carried away small bits of rock and minerals, known as sediment. Sediment settled in several large valleys between Wyoming's mountains. Most of the sediment, however, was carried out of the state. Today, most of Wyoming has only a thin layer of poor soil, which supports a narrow range of plant life.

WORD TO KNOW

erosion *the gradual wearing away of rock or soil by physical breakdown, chemical solution, or water*

Wyoming Geo-Facts

Along with the state's geographical highlights, this chart ranks Wyoming's land, water, and total area compared to all other states.

Total area; rank . . . . . 97,814 square miles (253,337 sq km); 10th
Land; rank . . . . 97,100 square miles (251,488 sq km); 9th
Water; rank . . . . 713 square miles (1,847 sq km); 36th
Inland water; rank . . . . 713 square miles (1,847 sq km); 30th
Geographic center . . . . Fremont, 58 miles (93 km)
east-northeast of Lander
Latitude . . . . 41° N to 45° N
Longitude . . . . 104°3' W to 111°3' W
Highest point . . . . Gannett Peak, 13,809 feet (4,209 m),
in Fremont County
Lowest point . . . . Belle Fourche River, 3,099 feet (945 m),
in Crook County
Largest city . . . . Cheyenne
Longest river . . . . North Platte River

Source: U.S. Census Bureau

All of the New England states (Maine, New Hampshire, Vermont, Massachusetts, Rhode Island, and Connecticut) plus New Jersey and Maryland could fit inside Wyoming!

Wyoming Topography

Use the color-coded elevation chart to see on the map Wyoming's
high points (dark red to orange) and low points (green to dark green).
Elevation is measured as the distance above or below sea level.

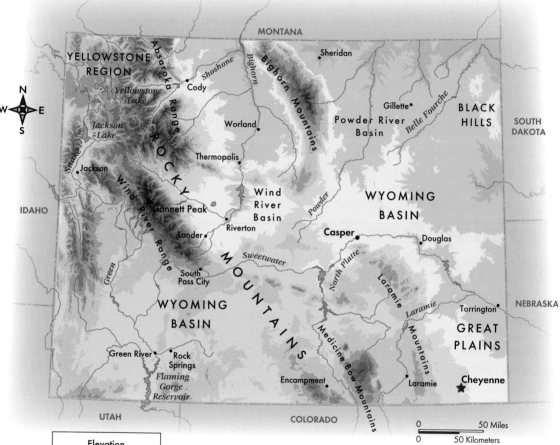

Elevation		
Feet		**Meters**
13,000		3,962
11,000		3,353
9,000		2,743
7,000		2,134
5,000		1,524

LAND REGIONS

Wyoming has four main land regions. The eastern one-
third of the state falls within the Great Plains, an area
of fairly level, mostly treeless spaces that stretches
all the way from Texas to northern Canada. The
Rocky Mountains cover much of western Wyoming.
The Wyoming Basins—wide valleys ringed by hills or
mountains—are found in the western and central part

Cattle grazing on the Great Plains of Wyoming

of the state. The Yellowstone Region, a place like no other in the world, is located in Wyoming's northwestern corner.

The Great Plains

The western part of the Great Plains, where Wyoming is located, is high and dry. It has an average elevation of 5,000 feet to 6,000 feet (1,500 m to 1,800 m). Hardy grasses cover most of Wyoming's Great Plains. The land is used mainly for cattle and sheep ranching. These animals graze on the wide, grassy plains.

Some parts of Wyoming's Great Plains support farms. Here farmers use **irrigation** to water their crops. The North Platte Valley and other agricultural areas separate Wyoming's southern plains from its northern plains. The northern plains lie among the Black Hills to the northeast, the Big Horn Mountains to the west,

WORD TO KNOW

irrigation *watering land by artificial means to promote plant growth*

and the Platte Valley to the south. The central part of Wyoming's Great Plains region consists of rolling prairies and stretches of sand.

The Rocky Mountains

The Rocky Mountain chain, which stretches from Mexico to Canada, goes through Wyoming. From the northwestern corner of the state, near Yellowstone National Park, the Rockies run southeast into Colorado. Several mountain ranges make up this section of the Rockies. They are the Absaroka, Teton, Gros Ventre, Owl Creek, Wind River, Big Horn, and Sierra Madre ranges. The state's highest point—Gannett Peak—stands in the Wind River Range. In Wyoming, the Rockies have many high peaks topped with snow. Streams rush down the mountainsides, carving canyons and creating waterfalls and lakes.

The Laramie and Medicine Bow mountain ranges, with peaks that reach from 10,000 to 12,000 feet (3,000 to 3,600 m), are located in southeastern Wyoming. The lower-lying Black Hills cross into the northeastern part of Wyoming from South Dakota. On average, they stand only about 6,000 feet (1,800 m) high. Covered with thick stands of ponderosa pines, they look black from a distance.

The Big Horn Mountain Range is located in the north-central part of the state. This range has more than a dozen peaks that vary in altitude from 9,000 feet (2,700 m) to more than 13,000 feet (4,000 m). Pine, fir, and spruce cover the lower levels of the Big Horn Mountains.

The Continental Divide runs through western Wyoming. Waterways to the east of the divide flow toward the Atlantic Ocean, and waterways to the west

SEE IT HERE!

DEVILS TOWER

The state's most recognizable landmark is found in the Great Plains region. Located in the northeastern corner of the state, Devils Tower is a massive pillar of **igneous** rock. It was formed millions of years ago when hot **magma** pushed upward into layers of **sedimentary** rock. The magma cooled and hardened as it approached the earth's surface. Over millions of years, the sedimentary rock eroded, leaving only the igneous rock showing. Today, the summit is 5,112 feet (1,558 m) above sea level. For many Native Americans, who call it Bear Lodge, Devils Tower is a sacred site. In 1906, Devils Tower became the first national monument in the United States.

WORDS TO KNOW

igneous *formed by the hardening of melted rock*

magma *melted rock that has not yet erupted*

sedimentary *formed from clay, sand, and gravel that settled at the bottom of a body of water*

flow to the Pacific. Two major western rivers have their sources in Wyoming's mountains. The Snake River starts in Yellowstone National Park, and the Green River starts in the Wind River Range.

The Wyoming Basins

Three major basins lie among Wyoming's tall mountain ranges. The Big Horn Basin is a fertile area in northwestern Wyoming. It's about 80 miles (130 km) wide and 100 miles (160 km) long. The Big Horn River and its **tributaries** run through the basin. Their waters make it possible for farmers to grow many crops in the basin. In the southwestern part of the state, the Green River Basin has many tree-lined streams. This area attracted fur trappers and traders in the early 1800s. It is also one of Wyoming's best farming areas.

WORD TO KNOW

tributaries *smaller rivers that flow into a larger river*

YELLOWSTONE
NATIONAL PARK

Established in 1872, Yellowstone National Park was the world's first national park. It's larger than Rhode Island and Delaware combined! Its 2.2 million acres (890,000 ha) offer visitors a wide range of sights and adventures. It has more **geysers** than anywhere else on Earth. It is known for its spectacular canyons, beautiful waterfalls, and unspoiled lakes and streams. Yellowstone is home to bison, grizzly bears, elk, moose, wolves, and many other animals. Nearly 3.1 million people visited Yellowstone in 2008.

WORDS TO KNOW

geothermal *relating to or produced by the heat of Earth's core*

geysers *springs that shoot steam and hot water from underground into the air*

The state's largest basin, the Great Divide Basin, sits north of the Sierra Madre range in the south-central part of the state. The Great Divide Basin is much different from the Big Horn and Green River basins. It sits at a very high elevation. It is so dry that most rain or snow evaporates before it reaches the ground. Because of the lack of water, there are no farms in the Great Divide Basin. Sheep from local ranches munch on the region's many sagebushes.

The Great Divide Basin is part of the Red Desert. Spreading for 6 million acres (2.4 million hectares) across southwestern Wyoming, the Red Desert is one of the largest cold deserts in the United States. What little water cold deserts get is in the form of snow. One section of the Red Desert, the Killpecker Sand Dunes, consists of huge dunes up to 150 feet (46 m) high.

The Yellowstone Region

Located in the northwestern corner of Wyoming, the Yellowstone Region is truly unique. It has high waterfalls, deep canyons, and many **geothermal** marvels. The Yellowstone River flows through the Yellowstone Canyon. The river plunges over Yellowstone Falls. The 308-foot-tall (94 m) Lower Yellowstone Falls is the park's highest waterfall. Mineral deposits have created pools of many different colors, including red, yellow, and blue.

Yellowstone National Park makes up most of the Yellowstone Region. It is home to about 10,000 geothermal features, created by millions of years of geological forces. Much of Yellowstone sits inside the crater of an active volcano. The last major eruption of this volcano occurred more than 600,000 years ago. Today, molten (hot melted) rock sits as close as 2 miles

HOW DOES A GEYSER WORK?

Hot molten rock close to the earth's surface heats a nearby pool of underground water. When the pool reaches the boiling point, steam and hot water shoot up a vent (tube) and spurt into the air. Cooler underground water refills the pool, and the process begins again. Yellowstone's Old Faithful geyser erupts about every hour for two to five minutes.

Tourists watch as Old Faithful erupts at Yellowstone National Park.

(3 km) from the surface. This molten rock heats water underneath the surface. The hot water creates spouting geysers and pools of bubbling mud that are known as mud pots.

Yellowstone is home to more than 500 geysers. That's about half of all the geysers in the world! They are found only in areas that have both volcanic activity and underground pools of water with vents to the surface.

Cross-country skiing is a popular pastime during Wyoming's snowy months.

CLIMATE

Wyoming has a mostly cool, dry, and windy climate. Because of its high elevation, temperatures in most of Wyoming are relatively cool in the summer and cold in the winter, especially in the mountains. Summer temperatures at lower elevations can be blistering.

Wyoming's mountains affect where it rains and snows. The mountains can trap storm clouds moving in from the west. Rain and snow often fall heavily in the mountains, but that usually leaves the eastern part of the state dry, with some areas seeing as little as 2 inches (5 centimeters) per year.

In March 2007, a powerful snowstorm dumped several feet of snow on Wyoming. Hobbs Park, near Lander, was buried under 58 inches (147 cm) of snow. High winds accompanied the snow-storm. At Buffalo, winds were measured at 65 mph (105 kph). The wind and snow com-bined to cause a bliz-zard, a severe weather condition that occurs when low tempera-tures, high winds, and falling or blowing snow combine to reduce visibility greatly. Blizzards are common in Wyoming.

Weather Report

This chart shows record temperatures (high and low) for the state, as well as average temperatures (July and January) and average annual precipitation.

Record high temperature . . . . .115°F (46°C) at Basin
on August 8, 1983

Record low temperature . . . . –66°F (–54°C) near Moran
on February 9, 1933

Average July temperature .71°F (22°C)
Average January temperature . . . . 20°F (–7°C)
Average yearly precipitation . . . . .13 inches (33 cm)

Source: National Climatic Data Center, NESDIS, NOAA, U.S. Department of Commerce

PLANT LIFE

From the Great Plains to the Rocky Mountains, Wyo-ming has many different environments for plant life. More than 2,500 plant species live in the state. Forests cover about one-sixth of Wyoming. At higher eleva-tions, where rain or snow falls, evergreen trees cover the land. These include tall lodgepole pines, Douglas fir, Engelmann spruce, and alpine firs. Ponderosa pines dominate the few forested parts of eastern Wyoming. Small patches of cottonwood trees, aspens, and bur oak grow near rivers, springs, and other moist places.

Wyoming's timberline is around 9,500 feet (2,900 m). That means no trees grow at elevations higher than this. Above the timberline, grasses, mosses, and flowers such as buttercups, forget-me-nots, and goldenrod grow. There are few trees in the Great Plains region, but many different types of grasses cover the ground. Bluestem, buffalo grass, and needlegrass are

Forget-me-not blossoms

Trumpeter swans in Jackson

common. Sagebrush grows in most parts of Wyoming, from deserts to mountains. Sagebrush thrives in Wyoming because it grows well in poor soil and dry climates. More than seven different species of sage grow in the state, including black sage and salt sage, but not the kind of sage that is used as an herb for cooking.

ANIMAL LIFE

About 300 species of birds live in or pass through Wyoming. Many types of birds of prey live in the state, including the bald eagle, Cooper's hawk, and prairie falcon. The black-billed magpie, yellow warbler, and meadowlark (the state bird) are three types of songbirds that live in Wyoming. Sage grouse, a bird similar to a chicken, live in sagebrush lands. Sage grouse can be found in every county in the state. Large trumpeter swans glide on Yellowstone Lake. Among Wyoming's 26

Wyoming National Park Areas

This map shows some of Wyoming's national parks, monuments, preserves, and other areas protected by the National Park Service.

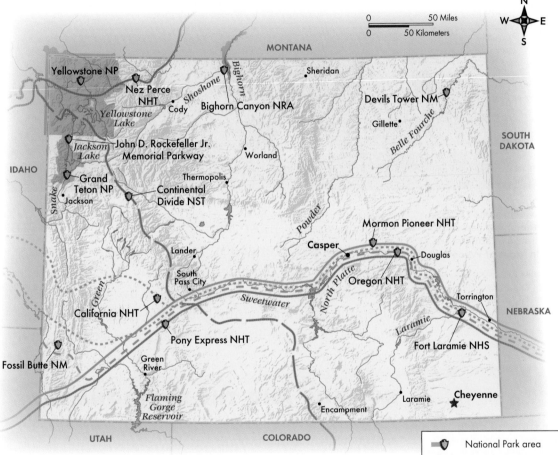

reptile species are two types of venomous rattlesnakes. Prairie rattlesnakes live in elevations below 7,000 feet (2,100 m). They can grow to more than 3 feet (1 m) long. The midget faded rattlesnake, which lives in the Green River Basin, is much smaller in size. Its venom, however, is more than 10 times stronger than the prairie rattler's!

Moose, which can weigh some 1,600 pounds (726 kilograms) and can sport 50-pound (23 kg) racks of antlers, are abundant in certain areas of Wyoming.

Are you taller than an elk's antlers? The antlers of a male elk can measure 5 feet (1.5 m) in height!

The state's most abundant large mammals are mule deer and pronghorn. Elk, bighorn sheep, moose, wolves, coyotes, and black and grizzly bears, as well as a few hundred bison (buffalo), also live in Wyoming. Common smaller mammals include foxes, jackrabbits, beavers, otters, yellow-bellied marmots, gophers, and prairie dogs.

HUMANS AND THE ENVIRONMENT

Wyoming's two biggest environmental concerns are scarce water and poor air quality. Runoff from cattle feedlots threatens many waterways. Rainwater carries livestock waste into streams and rivers, polluting sources of drinking water. The expansion of oil and natural gas wells endangers unspoiled landscapes, particularly in the Red Desert and the Bridger-Teton National Forest. Benzene and other harmful gases are released during the construction and operation of oil and gas wells. To reduce the levels of pollutants released

JILL MORRISON: COMMUNITY ORGANIZER

Jill Morrison (1959–) works with local residents, government officials, and other environmentalists to help preserve the environment of the Powder River Basin. Oil and natural gas drilling, coal mining, and other industrial activities in the region have caused widespread erosion, water pollution, and soil damage. Morrison is a community organizer for the Powder River Basin Resource Council. She helps ranchers and other landowners prevent industrial damage to their land, water resources, and traditional way of life.

 Want to know more? See www.leadership forchange.org/awardees/awardee.php3?ID=223

ENDANGERED ANIMALS

The U.S. Fish and Wildlife Service lists eight animal species and three plant species in Wyoming as **endangered** or **threatened**. The black-footed ferret is an endangered species of special concern in Wyoming. These ferrets once lived in grasslands and basins from Texas to Canada. They depended on prairie dog towns for food and shelter. Prairie dogs ate vast stretches of grass that ranchers wanted for their cows and sheep, so the ranchers destroyed most prairie dog towns. As prairie dog towns disappeared, so did the ferrets.

Thought to have been extinct, black-footed ferrets were discovered in a prairie dog town near Meeteetse in north-central Wyoming in 1981. Scientists captured 18 surviving members in 1987 and started a breeding program. The offspring of these 18 ferrets were released back into the wild in the Shirley Basin in 1991. Today, the Shirley Basin colony is one of several black-footed ferret colonies in the United States. It now has more than 300 ferrets. Despite these efforts, the black-footed ferret remains one of the world's rarest mammals.

Black-footed ferret

into the air and the state's water supplies, Wyoming residents have joined together to urge the state legislature to increase regulation of feedlots and oil and gas wells.

The Wyoming legislature set up a state agency, the Environmental Quality Council, to decide all cases involving state environmental regulations. Seven people, who are appointed by the governor, sit on the council's board. In 2008, the council took action against a uranium mine near Douglas. It ordered the mine company to reduce its spills and to comply with other state environmental laws. Many Wyomingites believe that, with efforts such as these, Wyoming may be able to preserve its natural heritage.

WORDS TO KNOW

endangered *at risk of becoming extinct*

threatened *likely to become endangered in the foreseeable future*

READ ABOUT

This Shoshone painting on animal hide shows a ceremonial dance after a hunt.

▲ **c. 10,000** BCE
The first humans arrive in present-day Wyoming

c. 7000 BCE
Climate change forces people out of Wyoming

c. 5000 BCE
People return to Wyoming in small numbers

CHAPTER TWO

FIRST PEOPLE

★

S CIENTISTS THINK THAT HUMANS FIRST CAME TO NORTH AMERICA DURING AN ICE AGE SOME 20,000 YEARS AGO. At this time, the Asian and North American landmasses were linked. People walked from Russia to Alaska, following game animals. The descendants of these early people slowly spread across the continent and arrived in what is now Wyoming about 12,000 years ago.

Shoshone water jug

▲ **1500s CE**
Shoshones first arrive in Wyoming

1700s
Arapahos and Cheyennes arrive in Wyoming

1800s
Sioux settle in Wyoming

Early peoples hunted a type of large bison that no longer exists today.

WORD TO KNOW

archaeologists *people who study the remains of past human societies*

EARLY WYOMINGITES

The first people to arrive in Wyoming found a land with high mountains and vast, treeless plains. Huge herds of mastodons, mammoths, and giant bison ate the region's abundant grasses. These mammals were much bigger than today's animals. The horns of today's bison are about 2 feet (0.6 m) long, but the horns of the giant bison stretched 6 feet (1.8 m) or more. **Archaeologists** believe that Wyoming's early residents hunted these beasts using spears with stone tips. These people lived in small groups, or bands, of about 20 to 50 members. It would have taken more than one hunter to bring down such a large animal and even more people to turn the prey into food, clothing, and useful objects.

Stone spear points have been found in Wyoming with the bones of mammoths and giant bison. These spear points date to about 9000 BCE. Scientists have also found large piles of animal bones at the foot of cliffs, at the bottom of steep gullies, and in sandpits. They believe that early hunters killed animals by chasing herds over cliffs or into gullies. They also herded their prey into places with deep sand. There the animals would get stuck, making it easier to kill them with a spear.

These hunters used quartzite and other types of stones to make weapons and tools. Quartzite and similar rocks are easy to chip. By breaking the stones, hunters could produce sharp edges. Early hunters used these sharp stones to make spear points, arrowheads, knives, scrapers, and other tools. The stones came from quarries in Goshen, Niobrara, and Platte counties in eastern Wyoming. In these three counties, there are many holes measuring about 20 feet (6 m) across and 15 to 20 feet (4.5 to 6 m) deep. Soil and broken rock are piled next to the holes. Early miners created this debris while digging for quartzite and other stones.

Around 7000 BCE, the climate in North America changed. The temperatures increased and rainfall decreased, causing Wyoming's grasslands to dry up. The huge mammals that the early Wyomingites had hunted for centuries became extinct. Wyoming's hunters followed deer and smaller bison to new grazing lands. Archaeologists have found no evidence of human life in Wyoming between about 7000 BCE and 5000 BCE. They believe that few people lived in or visited Wyoming during those 2,000 years.

Scientists believe that the climate changed again around 5000 BCE. With cooler and wetter weather, the region once again became livable for animals and

THE SPANISH DIGGINGS

Cowboys discovered the quarries of the earliest Wyomingites in the 1870s. They called them the Spanish Diggings. They believed Spanish explorers in the 1500s had dug them searching for gold. It never occurred to the cowboys that these quarries were Native American mining sites.

FAQ

Q8 WHAT CAUSED THE EXTINCTION OF HUGE MAMMALS LIKE THE GIANT BISON?

A8 Some scientists believe that overhunting by humans caused their extinction. Others believe that a major cooling in North America's climate wiped out the plants that these animals ate.

Native American Peoples

(Before European Contact)

This map shows the general area of Native American peoples before European settlers arrived.

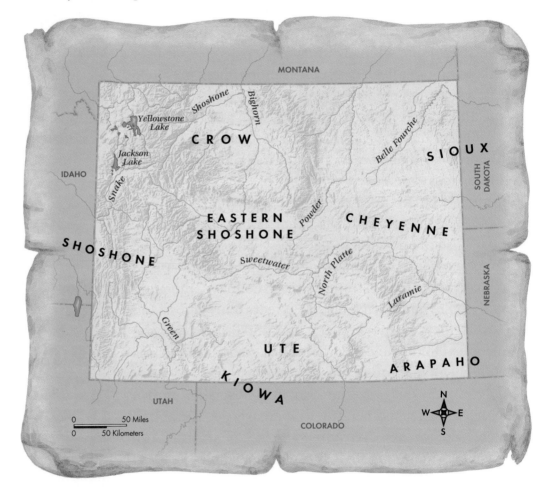

humans. Archaeologists have found many sites inhabited by humans around 4500 BCE. Most people came to Wyoming to mine quartzite and left once they had dug up what they needed. Harsh winters and rugged terrain made Wyoming uninviting. The soil was too poor to farm, and the hunting was more plentiful to the east and south. Wyoming would remain sparsely populated for more than 6,000 years.

THE SHOSHONE PEOPLE

Beginning in the 1500s, small bands of hunters began moving into Wyoming from the north and west, from what is now Idaho and Montana. They traveled through the Big Horn, Powder, and Tongue river basins. Today, these people are known as the Shoshone Nation. The name Shoshone was used for several different Native American groups. Only the Eastern, or Wind River, Shoshone settled in Wyoming. They lived in small **nomadic** bands of people, most of whom were related to each other. Wind River Shoshones hunted game, particularly pronghorn, in the Grand Teton and Wind River mountains.

The lives of the Shoshone and all **Plains Indians** changed completely with the arrival of horses, which Spanish explorers had introduced to the American West. When they obtained horses in the late 1600s, the Plains Indians began to hunt bison on the plains.

SEE IT HERE!

MEDICINE WHEEL

A mysterious ring of stones known as the Medicine Wheel sits in the Big Horn Mountains west of Sheridan. The large circle measures 143 feet (44 m) in diameter. A cairn, or pile of stones, lies in the center of the circle. Twenty-eight rows of stones shoot out from the cairn like the spokes of a wheel. Scientists believe that Native Americans arranged the stones as early as 1200. No one is sure why or how the site was used. Some archaeologists believe that the site was used for religious purposes. Others believe that Indians used the site as a calendar. The cairn represented the sun, and the 28 "spokes" represented the 28 days in a lunar month.

Shoshone hunting party

WORDS TO KNOW

nomadic *describing someone who moves from place to place and does not permanently settle in one location*

Plains Indians *nations of bison hunters who lived from the Mississippi River west to the Rockies and from Texas north to central Canada*

AWARD-WINNING SCULPTOR

Lewis "Bud" Boller (1928–) is an award-winning sculptor. His artworks focus on Western themes and often portray Native Americans, cowboys, or wildlife. His work is noted for its realistic style, which conveys the spirit of his subjects. He received a Wyoming Governor's Arts Award in 1995. Before becoming an artist, Boller worked as a rodeo cowboy and as a rancher. A member of the Shoshone Nation, he lives on a ranch on the Wind River Indian Reservation.

Picture Yourself . . .

Building a Tipi with Your Crow Family

To make a tipi, you and your mother first build the framework. You tie three or four long wooden poles together near their tops. You then spread out the bottom sections, or legs, of the poles as far as they will reach. Next, stack about a dozen poles against the framework, forming a large circle. To make the walls, you stretch large pieces of leather around the framework. You leave a flap open at the top and use long poles to keep it open. This creates a hole in the top of the tipi, allowing smoke from your fire to escape. Another flap at the bottom serves as the door. Finally, you arrange hides inside the walls of the tipi, and you've got a place to sleep.

Horses made hunting bison much easier. Several Shoshone bands joined together in spring for the bison hunt. In fall, they would split up for the winter and head back to the mountain valleys. During the winter, they gathered wild foods and hunted smaller animals.

THE CROW PEOPLE

The Crow people originally lived along the upper Missouri River in present-day North Dakota. They moved west in the 1400s. One group stayed in present-day southern Montana. Another group moved south into Wyoming, roaming the Big Horn, Powder River, and Wind River basins. They found plenty of animals to hunt and gathered wild fruits and vegetables to round out their diet.

Like other Plains Indians, the Crows moved their camps often, following herds of bison and other game. They and other Plains peoples lived in tipis, temporary structures made of wooden poles and animal skins, which were lightweight and easy to set up. For storage, they used lightweight baskets woven from

Tipis in a Crow encampment

the plentiful grasses. They made their clothing from animal hides, which were also lightweight and warm.

THE ARAPAHO PEOPLE

Arapahos originally lived in the Red River valley in Minnesota and North Dakota. These bison hunters moved west into present-day Montana and eventually into present-day Wyoming in

THE BEAUTY OF BISON

Plains Indians used almost every part of the bison. The animal provided meat, which they ate fresh or preserved, drying it in strips over a fire. Women turned the bison hides into leather, which they used to make tipi covers, shields, drums, robes, and rawhide straps. Men carved the bones into tools, cooking utensils, and ornaments. Hooves were made into ceremonial rattles or cooked to make glue. In winter, Native Americans stuffed their shoes with bison hair for warmth. They also used the hair to make balls for games and to make decorative ornaments. The plains had few trees, so what fuel did Plains Indians use in their fires? They burned bison dung!

Arapaho adults and children gather for a Sun Dance ceremony.

the late 1700s or early 1800s. The Northern Arapaho Nation settled along the headwaters of the Platte River, just east of the Rocky Mountains. They became known as expert horse trainers and riders.

One of the most important ceremonies to Arapahos and other Plains people was the Sun Dance ceremony. During the ceremony, members of secret warrior societies performed rituals around a tree trunk while gazing at the sun. The men believed that this could help influence events, such as warfare and hunting. Dancers sometimes went five days without food or sleep.

THE CHEYENNE PEOPLE

Like the Arapaho people, the Cheyenne Nation came to Wyoming from present-day North Dakota and Montana. At one time, they lived east of the Missouri River in what is now Minnesota. They were farmers who lived in permanent villages. They later moved west, perhaps pushed out by the Sioux and Chippewa people. They built villages and established farms along the Missouri River in present-day North Dakota.

When Cheyenne people obtained horses during the 1700s, they gave up farming, or "lost the corn," as a Cheyenne legend tells. They instead began hunting bison. To prepare for a hunt, the hunters performed the Animal Dance. Some men dressed as animals, and other men pretended to hunt them, herding them together. The ceremony lasted for five days.

In the early 1800s, the Cheyenne people moved farther west. They settled along what is now called the Cheyenne River, in the Black Hills. Sioux soon pushed

A Cheyenne woman uses a mortar and pestle to prepare wild cherries for pemmican, a mixture of meat and fruit.

them farther south to an area of the North Platte in present-day eastern Wyoming and western Nebraska. The Cheyenne people split into two groups. Only the Northern Cheyenne stayed in the North Platte region.

THE SIOUX PEOPLE

The Sioux originally lived in Wisconsin and Minnesota, along the northern section of the Mississippi River. By the 1700s, they began migrating westward as warfare with the Ojibwa people and the influx of Europeans threatened their homelands. In the early 19th century, a powerful group of Sioux called the Teton, or Lakota, Sioux moved to what is now eastern Wyoming and Montana and western South Dakota. The popular image of Native Americans—hunters on horseback

Sioux hunters in pursuit of bison

chasing bison across the Great Plains, the tipis, and the feathered warbonnets—is based on Sioux culture.

CONFLICTS ARISE

By the early 1800s, the Native peoples of Wyoming lived in stable communities. Horses had enabled the various nations to expand their hunting grounds, and their populations grew as food became more abundant. Horses also sped up the movement of people and goods. The Plains Indians established trade relationships with groups outside of the region. They also had more time for religious ceremonies and leisure activities. Each nation was a complex society with deep religious beliefs and practices.

Conflicts over land arose between groups. In the 1700s, Plains people acquired guns from Europeans, changing the nature of warfare. As raids to steal horses and armed conflicts grew, warrior-fighters became important to their nations. Some nations, particularly the Sioux and the Cheyenne, became military powers. They pushed weaker nations out of the best hunting grounds.

Several Indian nations were forced to leave their traditional lands. Some ended up in the largely unoccupied areas of Wyoming. The Blackfoot, Ute, Bannock, Modoc, and Kiowa nations settled in Wyoming for a while. They eventually moved on. The Crow people were pushed into the Big Horn Basin, and the Shoshone people fled to the mountainous western half of present-day Wyoming. Groups of Cheyenne, Arapaho, and Sioux held on to the more desirable land in the plains of eastern Wyoming. As explorers, trappers, miners, and settlers began making their way across Wyoming, Native Americans in the region would face even greater change.

Arapaho moccasins

36

A view from
the Wind River
Mountains,
mid-1800s

1803
*The Louisiana
Purchase transfers
much of Wyoming to
the United States*

1806 ▲
*John Colter arrives
in Wyoming*

1820s
*Mountain men come to
Wyoming to trap for furs*

CHAPTER THREE

EXPLORATION AND SETTLEMENT

★

BEFORE THE EARLY 1800s, ONLY NATIVE AMERICANS AND A FEW FRENCH FUR TRADERS LIVED IN WYOMING. A huge land deal would change that. In 1803, President Thomas Jefferson bought enough land from France to double the size of the United States overnight. Most of Wyoming was included in the sale, called the Louisiana Purchase. At the time, the region's population of Shoshone, Crow, Cheyenne, and Arapaho nations totaled about 10,000.

1840s
The era of the mountain men ends

1850 ▶
Fifty-five thousand people travel across Wyoming on the Oregon Trail

1860
Pony Express riders cross Wyoming

Exploration of Wyoming

The colored arrows on this map show the routes taken by explorers and pioneers between 1742 and 1824.

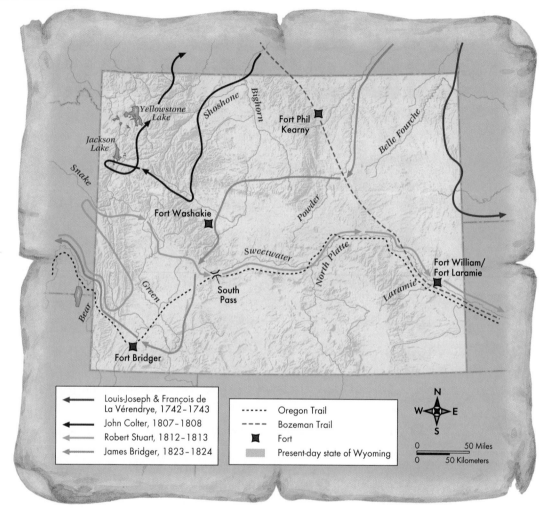

Louis-Joseph & François de La Vérendrye, 1742–1743
John Colter, 1807–1808
Robert Stuart, 1812–1813
James Bridger, 1823–1824

Oregon Trail
Bozeman Trail
Fort
Present-day state of Wyoming

FUR TRADERS

Sixty years before the Louisiana Purchase, two French-Canadian brothers, François and Louis-Joseph de La Vérendrye, had explored the northern plains. They wanted to trap and trade for animal furs and to find a route to the Pacific Ocean. Led by two Indian guides, the brothers and two servants headed westward from present-day North Dakota in July 1742. One of the brothers wrote in his journal that they had seen high mountains and traveled through "magnificent prairies" teeming with "wild animals." The brothers may have entered the northeast corner of what is now Wyoming.

After local Indians told them that there was no route to the Pacific, the La Vérendryes turned around. They went back to Canada and never returned to Wyoming. They had been the first Europeans to enter the area. It would be decades before others followed.

In 1804, President Jefferson directed two former army men, Meriwether Lewis and William Clark, to lead a group on an exploration of the Louisiana Purchase and lands west to the Pacific. John Colter was a member of that group. On the return trip in 1806, he left the expedition to guide a group of trappers. He became the first American known to have entered Wyoming when he led them to the region in search of beavers.

In spring 1807, Colter joined a trapping party, led by Spanish trader Manuel Lisa, through the Rocky Mountains. The Lisa expedition arrived at the junction of the Big Horn and Yellowstone rivers in October 1807. They built a trading post and began trapping animals. Colter traveled to Crow villages to invite the Indians to the new trading post. He also wanted to hire Indian guides. While seeking out new villages to trade with,

Q8 WHAT AREA WAS INCLUDED IN THE LOUISIANA PURCHASE?

A8 The Louisiana Purchase included all the land between the Mississippi River and the Rocky Mountains.

Louisiana Purchase

This map shows the area (in yellow) that made up the Louisiana Purchase and the present-day state of Wyoming (in orange).

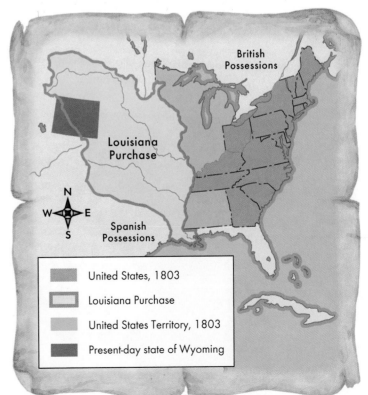

MINI-BIO

JOHN COLTER: TRAPPER AND GUIDE

John Colter (c. 1773?–1813) was the first known European American to set foot in Wyoming. Born in Virginia, Colter left the Lewis and Clark expedition in 1806 to guide trappers around the northern Rockies. He spent much of the winter of 1806–1807 exploring the Wyoming region, most of it alone. Colter made a legendary escape from a group of Blackfoot Indians, who were trying to drive him from the region. They stripped off his clothes and forced him to run for his life. He eluded his pursuers for seven days, making his way through rugged terrain back to a trappers' camp.

? Want to know more? See http://xroads.virginia.edu/~hyper/hns/mtmen/johncol.html

he became the first person of European descent to see the spouting geysers and steaming pools of the Yellowstone region.

Three years later, the American Fur Company sent Wilson Price Hunt to lead an expedition to the company's trading post in Astoria, Oregon. Hunt led 62 men, one woman, and two children across Wyoming. To avoid the Blackfoot in Montana, Hunt led his party through the Big Horn and the Wind River mountain ranges. They went through Union Pass (near present-day Dubois) and

Trapper Jedediah Smith being attacked by a grizzly bear

descended into the Green River valley in September 1811. Hunt wrote in his journal that the Green River appeared to be "very favorable for hunting beaver." On the other side of the Gros Ventre Mountains, the party traded with Shoshones for beaver pelts. The party continued into Jackson Hole. After great hardship, they finally made it to Astoria in February 1812.

In June 1812, a seven-man party led by Robert Stuart left Astoria, heading east. Arriving in St. Louis, Missouri, they reported that Wyoming had beaver to be trapped, but mostly they talked about the rugged mountains that they had to pass over.

MOUNTAIN MEN

The fur trade in Wyoming was slow at first. Trapping was hard work. A trapper had to travel across a wide area to find good beaver ponds. He had to carry about six 5-pound (2 kg) traps for long distances and wade into ice-cold ponds to set the traps. He had to check the traps, skin any animals that he caught, and carry the pelts back to camp. The work was also very dangerous. In addition to dealing with challenging weather conditions, trappers were constantly on guard for attacks by grizzly bears or wolves. Once, a grizzly attacked trapper Jedediah Smith, inflicting serious wounds. One of his men had to sew one of Smith's ears back on! Trappers worked hundreds of miles from forts and supplies. They hunted or gathered most of their food. Trappers sometimes ate insects, killed their dogs for meat, or even chewed on leather to lessen hunger pangs. They endured freezing weather.

Wyoming's fur trade began to grow in the 1820s. William Ashley employed many of the traders. One of his ads in a St. Louis newspaper sought "100 Enterprising

FAQ

Q: WHAT IS A "HOLE"?
**A: ** Early fur trappers called some valleys "holes" because they had to climb down very steep mountains to reach them.

WYOMING'S FUR TRADE

Most of the fur trade in the United States involved traders from afar swapping clothes, tools, and weapons with Indians for beaver pelts. In Wyoming and nearby areas, however, white men did most of the trapping. A number of African Americans were also prominent in the trade, most notably James Beckwourth and Edward Rose. Beckwourth became a chief of the Crow Nation, and Rose forged a reputation for getting along with various Native American nations.

James Beckwourth

Picture Yourself . . .

as a Mountain Man

If you were a mountain man heading into Wyoming's wilderness, how would you dress and what gear would you take? For underwear, you wear a red flannel **loincloth** underneath deerskin leggings. Your trousers and jacket are also made of deerskin. The long, fringed jacket extends below your knees. You slip a pair of moccasins made out of buffalo or deer leather onto your feet. A leather belt holds up your trousers. A wool or deerskin hat sits atop your head.

You have to carry all the gear you need to survive. You stick your pistol, knife, and hatchet in your belt. You loop your powder horn and bullet pouch over your shoulders so they hang by your side. You pack the rest of your gear on your horse or mule. Heavy boots, cooking gear, and basic foods, such as coffee, salt, and pemmican (dried meat), are a must. Finally, you load your five or six beaver traps. You're ready to go! Grab your flintlock rifle and head out for a season of trapping.

WORD TO KNOW

loincloth *a strip of cloth or leather worn between the legs that passes over a belt or cord tied around the waist*

Young Men" to travel up the Missouri River to trap furs for him. They later became known as mountain men. To avoid the Blackfoot farther north in Montana, Ashley's men focused on trapping furs in the Green River and the Big Horn River valleys. The first group of Ashley's men to go through South Pass included Jedediah Smith, Jim Bridger, and William Sublette. They found excellent trapping along the Green River.

In the mid-1820s, Ashley arranged a yearly gathering of mountain men on the Green River. It allowed his company to buy beaver pelts from the trappers without having to build, maintain, and defend remote trading posts. Mountain men traded their pelts to fur buyers for money and supplies. For the mountain men, each year's gathering, or rendezvous, meant more than just getting paid for their furs. Working as a fur trapper was a solitary job, and most trappers barely earned a living. But for about two weeks every June or July during the rendezvous, the mountain men enjoyed abundant food and trading tall tales with their fellow trappers.

By the early 1840s, Wyoming's mountain men had hunted local beaver populations nearly to extinction. Most trappers moved on, but some stayed to start guide businesses or become ranchers or miners. Despite their small numbers, Wyoming's mountain men had played an important role in opening up the West for American settlement. They learned about the region's geography, weather, wildlife, and plant life. They would pass this valuable knowledge along to thousands of settlers heading west. They also grew to better understand Native American ways. They befriended Indians, and many mountain men married Indian women.

A group of trappers heads out for a beaver hunt, mid-1800s.

MINI-BIO

JIM BRIDGER: MOUNTAIN MAN

Born in Virginia, Jim Bridger (1804–1881) headed west as a boy and joined his first trapping expedition at 18. He explored a large area from the Missouri River west to Utah and Idaho. He learned several Indian languages and served as a scout for the U.S. Army. With Louis Vasquez, he established Fort Bridger, a trading post in southwestern Wyoming. It later became a military base but was shut down in 1890.

? Want to know more? See http://xroads.virginia.edu/~hyper/hns/mtmen/jimbrid.html

The mountain men did not threaten the existence of the Native American nations in Wyoming, though they had a sometimes devastating effect on individual villages. The impending flood of settlers across the plains, however, would change the lives of the Native Americans forever.

THE OREGON TRAIL

Starting in 1840, thousands of families from the eastern states made the long, difficult journey along the Oregon Trail, which cut across Wyoming. Their heavy wagons were packed with food, clothing, and other possessions. Adults and older children walked alongside the wagon. One traveler wrote in 1846: "I see nothing but big rocks, high mountains, and wild sage. . . . It is a miserable country."

People moved west for a variety of reasons. A financial panic in 1837 had caused many Americans to lose their jobs. Others wanted to get out of the crowded,

This image by German American painter Albert Bierstadt shows wagons on the Oregon Trail.

polluted cities. Residents of the eastern states heard exaggerated stories that a new, better life could be found in the territories of California and Oregon. These regions offered good farmland and a warm, sunny climate. In 1847, members of the Church of Jesus Christ of Latter-day Saints established their own territory in the Great Salt Lake Valley in present-day Utah. Thousands of Mormons, as they were widely known, began to stream across Wyoming.

In 1849, the discovery of gold in California prompted another wave of travelers to cross Wyoming. Between 1841 and 1868, more than 350,000 people, mostly men, moved through Wyoming. The traffic peaked in 1850 (55,000) and 1852 (50,000). Gold discoveries in Idaho and Montana increased the flow of people in 1865 and 1866.

The best overland route to the West Coast went through Wyoming. From Independence, Missouri, settlers followed the Platte and North Platte rivers across present-day Nebraska into what is now central Wyoming. This part of the trail stretched about 600 miles (1,000 km). Passing over the Great Plains, it was relatively smooth and dry most of the time. The tree-lined rivers provided water and grass for livestock and wood for cooking fires. From the North Platte, the trail followed the Sweetwater River, which ran 100 miles (161 km) through the Great Divide Basin to South Pass. Sitting at an elevation of only 7,500 feet (2,286 m), South Pass was by far the easiest place to cross the rugged Rocky Mountains. After South Pass, the Oregon Trail headed west across present-day Wyoming, Idaho, and into Oregon.

It took about three to five weeks to pass through Wyoming. The pioneers grew weary of the dry land,

A TWO-WAY ROAD

Originally called the Platte River Road (or simply "the Road"), the Oregon Trail ran from Independence, Missouri, to Oregon City, Oregon. The Road was actually a series of different trails. It became known as the Oregon Trail because its first travelers were headed to the Oregon Territory. But not all of the traffic headed west. Unsuccessful miners came back on the trail. Mormons returned east for supplies and to guide more members of their faith to Utah. Soldiers, settlers, stagecoach passengers, Pony Express riders, cowboys, and telegraph company employees all traveled back and forth over the trails.

the blowing sand, and the endless sagebrush. They endured bad weather, high winds, dust storms, insect bites, and hunger. Wagons broke down. Livestock died. Families often had to abandon their prized possessions to lighten the load for the oxen. The daily grind was tiring, and arguments broke out. People died from accidents, drowning, diseases, or winter storms. At Independence Rock, many people carved or painted their names into the stone to let later travelers know that they had passed that way. Today, Oregon Trail wagon tracks are still visible in Wyoming. Remnants of trading posts, graves, and artifacts are still being discovered along the trail.

To protect and supply the hordes of newcomers, the U.S. Army bought Fort Laramie, Fort Bridger, and other posts that had served fur trappers. Busy markets grew up around the forts. Here pioneers could buy flour, sugar, and other needed goods. They could also repair their wagons and trade for fresh oxen and horses.

Activity inside Fort Laramie

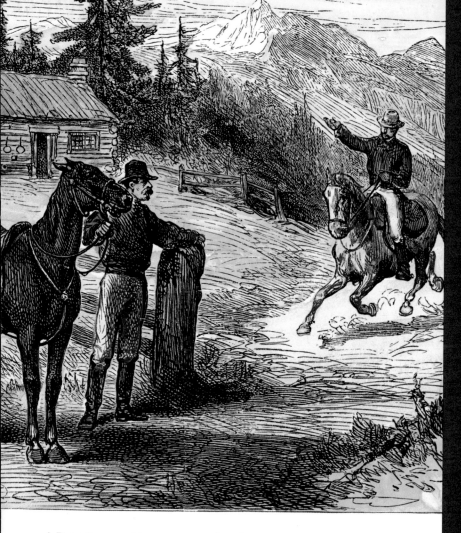

A Pony Express rider prepares to hand over the mail to the next rider.

THE PONY EXPRESS

The Pony Express was a mail service that ran between St. Joseph, Missouri, and Sacramento, California. Small men and boys weighing less than 125 pounds (57 kg) served as riders. They rode for about 10 miles (16 km) before changing horses, and every 30 miles (48 km) or so they handed the mail pouch to the next rider. It took 10 days for a mail pouch to make the trip between the two cities. More than 40 Pony Express stations were located in Wyoming, including at Fort Laramie and Fort Bridger. Pony Express service began in April 1860 but lasted only 18 months. Once telegraph lines crossed the country in October 1861, messages could be sent quickly and easily, and the Pony Express was no longer needed.

Apart from forts, however, Wyoming had virtually no other permanent towns. Very few people who passed through Wyoming decided to stay. To them, it was a barren stretch of trail on the way to their destination.

By the early 1860s, the population of Wyoming had not grown very much. Despite the heavy traffic on the Oregon Trail, only a few people had settled in the region. Some mountain men remained, working as guides or in other businesses. The rest of the white population was made up of soldiers stationed at forts and people who had started businesses supplying pioneers or operating toll ferries or bridges over rivers.

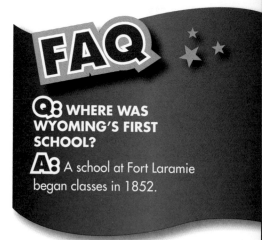

FAQ

Q8 WHERE WAS WYOMING'S FIRST SCHOOL?

A8 A school at Fort Laramie began classes in 1852.

Feeling threatened by the white settlers, Native Americans sometimes resorted to attacking wagon trains.

TENSIONS RISE

As the number of settlers passing through Wyoming increased, so did conflicts with Native Americans. Many Wyoming Indians became angry at how white pioneers were harming the land. Their livestock polluted streams and trampled and devoured grass. Pioneers killed more bison than they needed, wasting the meat. Whites soon found that Indians were stealing horses and attacking their wagon trains.

The Crow people were traditional enemies of the Sioux and Nez Percé peoples, but they all became allies against the tide of white settlers. In 1850, 10,000 Indians from different nations met in Laramie. The U.S.

government's local Indian agent, Thomas Fitzpatrick, asked their permission for settlers to use the Oregon Trail across Indian lands in Wyoming. The main purpose of the Fort Laramie Treaty of 1851 was to guarantee to Indians that if they didn't bother travelers along the trails, the government would make sure that travelers didn't get off the trail and trespass into Indian country.

The U.S. government promised to give each nation a yearly allotment of trade goods, such as food and cloth. In return, the nations would agree to stay within certain areas. They would also agree to punish any of their members who attacked white settlers. By offering food and other gifts, the government hoped that the Plains Indians would not see whites as invaders.

The agreements made at the Laramie meeting soon fell apart. With each new gold rush—California (1849), Colorado (1859), Montana (1864)—more settlers trespassed on Indian lands. They brought disease to the Indians, and they killed off the bison herds that nourished Indian communities. Native Americans responded by attacking the symbols of the invasion— wagon trains, stagecoaches, and farms. Many white Americans began demanding that the federal government find a solution to the "Indian problem." The impending arrival of the railroad in Wyoming would signal the beginning of the end of traditional Plains Indian life.

MINI-BIO

THOMAS FITZPATRICK: FUR TRAPPER

Born in Ireland, Thomas Fitzpatrick (1799–1854) became a fur trapper for William Ashley in 1823. In 1834, he left the fur business to become a guide, leading wagon trains over the Oregon Trail. The U.S. government appointed him as an Indian agent in 1846. In that role, he negotiated the Fort Laramie Treaty of 1851.

? Want to know more? See http://wildwest history.org/research/bios/Fitzpatrick_Thomas.asp

READ
ABOUT

Some travelers on the Oregon Trail decided to stay in the region that became Wyoming.

1861

Wyoming becomes part of the Dakota Territory

▲**1867**

Union Pacific Railroad tracks are laid in Wyoming

1869

Wyoming is organized as a territory

GROWTH AND CHANGE

★

WYOMING'S HARSH CLIMATE AND POOR SOIL DID NOT APPEAL TO MANY PIONEERS. But some people who passed through on the Oregon Trail decided to stay. By the mid-1860s, Wyoming's permanent white population was about 4,000. In 1867, one event sparked the settlement of Wyoming: the railroad arrived.

1877

The U.S. Army drives the Sioux out of Wyoming

1890 ▶

Wyoming becomes the 44th state

1903

A coal mine accident in Hanna claims the lives of 169 men

Laborers on the Union Pacific Railroad
working on a tunnel

THE UNION PACIFIC

In early 1867, Union Pacific Railroad crews laying track
westward from Omaha, Nebraska, reached the Wyoming
border. They built a depot in southeastern Wyoming,
and beside the depot they laid out streets for a town.
Railroad workers set up tents and built shacks. These
workers included immigrants from Ireland, China,
and elsewhere as well as white and black Americans.
Barbers, cooks, and business owners providing services
to the Union Pacific workers began to move in. By the
time the tracks reached the town, called Cheyenne, in
November, it had a population of 3,000. The first Union
Pacific train chugged into Cheyenne on November 13.
Within a year, the town's population rocketed to 6,000.
Almost the entire population was male.

The Union Pacific's chief engineer, Grenville M.
Dodge, had plotted a course that shot across southern

Wyoming, over the Laramie Mountains, across the plains and the Red Desert, and into northern Utah. As the track moved west, towns sprang up alongside it. They disappeared just as fast, as crews moved their tents west with the track. Dodge tried to plan the route to avoid disturbing Wyoming's Indians. But the Sioux, Cheyenne, and Arapaho nations threatened **surveyors** and other workers. They pulled up survey stakes and stole horses from the railroad crews. Bloody conflicts erupted between Indians and train crews. The U.S. Army sent soldiers to Wyoming to protect railroad workers.

When the Union Pacific crews reached Wyoming's Red Desert, they picked up their pace. Track workers set a record when they laid 7.5 miles (12 km) of track in one day. Meanwhile, crews for the Central Pacific Railroad Company had been laying track eastward from Sacramento, California, and were working their

SEE IT HERE!

CHEYENNE DEPOT MUSEUM
The original Cheyenne Depot, built in 1867, was a small wooden building. In 1887, a much grander Union Pacific Depot was built on the same site. Today it is a National Historic Landmark and a museum. It houses photos, displays, and artifacts about Cheyenne's founding, Union Pacific employees, and how the railroad spurred Wyoming's growth.

WORD TO KNOW

surveyors *people who measure land to set boundaries or mark building sites*

Pickax

WORKING ON THE RAILROAD

Railroad construction required different crews and a lot of labor. A crew of surveyors scouted ahead, finding the best path for the tracks to take. They pounded wooden stakes into the ground to mark the path. The next crews built bridges and dug tunnels for the tracks to pass over waterways and through mountains. Then came the grading crews. They used pickaxes and shovels to make the roadbed level. After that came the people who laid the ties, or wooden planks, that support the railroad tracks. Ties were laid about 2 feet (0.6 m) apart. Each layer of track used about 2,500 ties per mile! Next came the "rust eaters," who positioned 500-pound (227 kg) sections of iron rail over the ties. Another crew drove iron spikes to hold down the rail sections. They hammered in about 9,000 spikes per mile. The last crew bolted the long sections of rails to each other. Workers were paid $2.50 a day, or about $36.50 in today's dollars.

way through Utah. Seventy-five miles (121 km) west of Wyoming, the Union Pacific and Central Pacific crews met. On May 10, 1869, the last spike was pounded in at Promontory Summit in Utah. The transcontinental railroad—a railroad from one coast to the other—was complete. Wyoming was suddenly within only a few days' travel from either coast.

A NEW TERRITORY

Steam-powered trains chugged across Wyoming, carrying passengers back and forth. They stopped for fuel and supplies at Laramie, Green River, Evanston, and other growing towns along the track. Wyoming miners dug coal for locomotive engines. The demand for wooden railroad ties boosted the state's logging industry.

In 1861, most of Wyoming was made part of the Dakota Territory, along with what are now North Dakota and South Dakota. When the population of Wyoming's boomtowns soared, the residents of eastern Dakota

The creation of the railroad helped boost the logging industry in Wyoming.

Territory began to worry that Wyomingites would gain control of the territorial government. Dakota officials asked the U.S. Congress to divide the territory. In July 25, 1868, Congress voted to create Wyoming Territory from the western half of Dakota Territory and small parts of Utah and Idaho, which made it a rectangle. The following year, Wyoming Territory was officially organized.

William Bright, a South Pass City saloonkeeper, was elected to the territorial legislature and became president of the senate. At this time in Wyoming, men outnumbered women by six to one. Bright introduced a woman **suffrage** bill, which the territorial legislature passed. Some historians believe this was to encourage more women to move to the territory. On December 10, 1869, Wyoming Territory became the first and only place in the United States where women could vote.

THE INDIAN WARS

The Bozeman Trail led from southeastern Wyoming north into Montana gold rush territory, cutting across traditional Indian hunting grounds. Miners trespassed on Indian lands when they used this trail. In 1866, a Sioux chief named Red Cloud led a combined force of Sioux, Cheyenne, and Arapaho fighters to defend their livelihoods. For the next two years, his soldiers attacked

MINI-BIO

ESTHER MORRIS: FIRST WOMAN JUDGE

Esther H. Morris (1812–1902) was born in New York City. She and her husband moved to the gold mining town of South Pass City. In 1870, Morris was appointed justice of the peace of South Pass City, making her the first woman judge in the United States. She served as justice of the peace for eight months and tried more than two dozen cases. One statue of Morris represents Wyoming in the U.S. Capitol's National Statuary Hall Collection, and another stands in front of the Wyoming State Capitol in Cheyenne.

? **Want to know more?** See http://wyoarchives. state.wy.us

Wyoming is one of only three states whose boundaries are all straight lines. Neighboring Colorado and Utah are the other two.

WORD TO KNOW

suffrage *the right to vote*

A group of U.S. troops, led by General William Sherman, meet with Chief Red Cloud and other Native Americans for the signing of the Fort Laramie Treaty of 1868.

FAQ

Q8 HOW BIG IS THE WIND RIVER INDIAN RESERVATION?

A8 It is 2.2 million acres (890,000 ha).

invaders throughout northern Wyoming and southern Montana in what became known as Red Cloud's War. The U.S. government could not defeat Red Cloud's forces and agreed to a second Fort Laramie Treaty in 1868. Most Cheyenne and Arapaho people accepted a home in Dakota Territory. Shoshones, who had become allies of the U.S. Army, stayed in central Wyoming, where they had lived before white Americans entered the area. It became the Wind River Indian Reservation.

By 1877, the U.S. Army drove the last Sioux out of Wyoming and forced them to settle on a reservation in South Dakota. The federal government promised Northern Arapahos a reservation in Colorado but said they would have to wait. They told Shoshone leader Washakie that they were sending Northern Arapahos to the Wind River Indian Reservation until they had their own reservation. Washakie reluctantly agreed, but after many years, the temporary arrangement became permanent.

CATTLE COUNTRY

As bison herds were hunted to near extinction and Native Americans were forced out of the territory, Wyoming became attractive to more and more ranchers. They found land that was good for grazing and had adequate water supplies. With the completion of the transcontinental railroad in 1869, Wyoming ranchers could easily ship their cows and sheep to markets in other parts of the country. During the 1870s and 1880s, millions of cattle were herded into or through Wyoming. From the outside, the cattle business looked easy. All a person had to do was let the cattle loose to graze on Wyoming's plains and then drive them to market. Costs were low because ranchers used open range on land that was owned by the federal government without paying for it. The territory attracted many cattle investors, including a large number from England and Scotland. Cheyenne soon became a home for cattle barons.

WASHAKIE: SHOSHONE LEADER

Washakie (c. 1804–1900) became the leader of the Eastern Shoshone Nation in 1842. Under his leadership, Shoshones sought peace with the U.S. government. They sided with the U.S. Army against Sioux and Cheyennes in Red Cloud's War. Washakie urged his people to gain an education and cooperate with federal authorities. In 1900, Washakie was buried with U.S. military honors at Fort Washakie on the Wind River Indian Reservation.

? Want to know more? See http://wyoarchives.state.wy.us

WASHAKIE'S LAMENT

"The white man . . . cannot know the cramp we feel in this little spot, with the undying remembrance of the fact . . . that every foot of what you proudly call America, not very long ago belonged to the red man. . . . There was room enough for all his many tribes, and all were happy in their freedom. . . . [O]ur fathers were steadily driven out, or killed, and we, their sons, but sorry remnants of tribes once mighty, are cornered in little spots of earth all ours by right—cornered like guilty prisoners, and watched by men with guns, who are more than anxious to kill us off."

—Washakie, Shoshone leader

A cowboy herds cattle on a ranch in Pitchfork in Park County.

During these early years of ranching, cattle roamed the open range. Cattle ranchers sorted them out in annual spring and fall roundups. The spring roundup was mainly for branding calves. The fall roundup was for gathering cattle for shipment to market. Local ranchers divided up unbranded cows, called mavericks. Conflicts over ownership soon arose. The wealthiest cattlemen formed the Wyoming Stock Growers Association. The territorial government gave this group the power to hold roundups and to receive money from the sale of mavericks. They also had the sole authority to declare who were rustlers, or livestock thieves. That often turned out to be innocent small ranchers who were not members of the association.

The harsh winter of 1886–1887 killed thousands of cattle. Some wealthy cattlemen lost their entire herd. Others began having troubles with small ranchers, many of whom were former cowboys who had worked for the large outfits prior to going out on their own. Tensions exploded in 1892. Four men died in a battle when wealthy Cheyenne-based cattlemen invaded Johnson County and tried to wipe out operators of small ranches. The incident is known as the Johnson County War.

Still, the cattle business thrived. By 1885, more than 800,000 cattle grazed in Wyoming. Cattle drives, cowboys, and roundups became part of Wyoming's image. The cowboy became the symbol of the territory, inspiring books and songs. Cowboys of all races worked hard for a measly $30 a month (and food).

Sheep arrived in Wyoming in the 1870s. By 1900, about 6 million sheep had found a home on the range. Cattlemen bristled because sheep were eating their cattle's grass. Conflicts arose between cattlemen and sheep ranchers. Cattlemen hired thugs to murder shepherds. Three shepherds were murdered in the Spring Creek Raid, in north-central Wyoming, in 1909.

Branding irons

CATTLE BRANDING

Early ranchers used brands instead of fences to keep track of their cattle. A branding iron burned the owner's mark into each cow's hide. Today, ranchers use freeze branding instead. A supercooled branding iron is pressed against the hide, killing the hairs that come into contact with it. Only white hairs grow back, producing the branding iron's mark.

STATEHOOD

To apply for statehood, a territory needed a population of 60,000 and a **constitution**. In 1889, 55 men were elected to a convention that met in Cheyenne to write a constitution. Wyoming voters, including women, quickly approved it. The territory's representative in the U.S. House of Representatives, Joseph Carey, introduced a bill seeking statehood for Wyoming.

The House of Representatives passed Carey's bill. In the U.S. Senate, however, some people hesitated to

WORD TO KNOW

constitution *a written document that contains all the governing principles of a state or country*

Wyoming: From Territory to Statehood
(1869–1890)

This map shows the original Washington, Dakota, and Nebraska territories and the area (in yellow) that was organized as Wyoming Territory in 1869 and became the state of Wyoming in 1890.

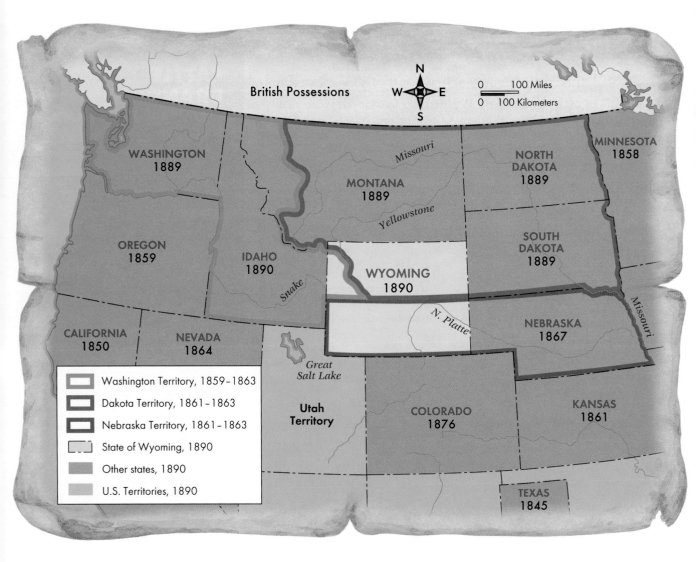

British Possessions

N
W E
S

0   100 Miles
0   100 Kilometers

WASHINGTON
1889

MONTANA
1889

Missouri

NORTH
DAKOTA
1889

MINNESOTA
1858

Yellowstone

OREGON
1859

IDAHO
1890

Snake

WYOMING
1890

SOUTH
DAKOTA
1889

N. Platte

NEBRASKA
1867

Missouri

CALIFORNIA
1850

NEVADA
1864

Great
Salt Lake

Utah
Territory

COLORADO
1876

KANSAS
1861

TEXAS
1845

Legend:
- Washington Territory, 1859–1863
- Dakota Territory, 1861–1863
- Nebraska Territory, 1861–1863
- State of Wyoming, 1890
- Other states, 1890
- U.S. Territories, 1890

Center Street in Casper, early 1900s

grant the territory statehood because Wyoming allowed women to vote. One senator claimed that women did not have the "capacity to vote wisely." Many senators agreed. They worried that other states might follow Wyoming's example. The Senate eventually passed the bill, and President Benjamin Harrison signed it into law on July 10, 1890. Wyoming was now a state, and Cheyenne its capital. In September, voters in Wyoming's first state election chose Francis E. Warren as their governor.

ECONOMIC GROWTH

Throughout the 1880s and 1890s, immigrants poured into Wyoming. Scandinavians settled in the agricultural regions of eastern Wyoming. Sugar beet farming in the Big Horn Basin and North Platte Valley attracted Mexican, German, and Russian immigrants. Workers

An oil well in Spring Valley

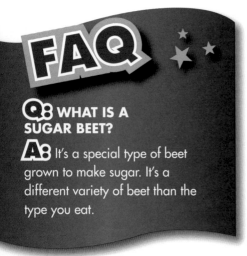

from Finland, Greece, Slovakia, and Italy came to work in the coal mines of Rock Springs and Sheridan. Scottish and English immigrants became cattle ranchers. Mormons from England and Denmark settled in the Big Horn Basin and southwestern Wyoming.

In 1883, Wyoming's first oil well was drilled at Dallas Dome, near Lander. In 1894, the state's first oil refinery opened near the biggest-producing oil fields, close to Casper. Wyoming oil companies sold most of their oil to the Union Pacific Railroad. By the early 1900s, the rising popularity of the automobile created a large, new market for oil products, such as gasoline. Oil wealth soon supported expensive restaurants and fancy hotels in Casper.

The 1890s also saw the rise of coal businesses. Coal mines had been established in Campbell, Uinta, Sweetwater, and Carbon counties when the railroad

FAQ

Q: WHAT IS A SUGAR BEET?

A: It's a special type of beet grown to make sugar. It's a different variety of beet than the type you eat.

was under construction in the 1860s. By the late 1880s, about 2,000 people worked in Wyoming's coal industry. At some mines, workers formed branches of the Knights of Labor, a successful **union**. Coal mining was hard and dangerous work. In 1903, 169 men were killed in a mine disaster at Hanna, Wyoming. Another 59 men died in the same mine five years later.

By 1900, Wyoming's population had grown to more than 92,000, but the state was still sparsely populated. Outlaws, such as Butch Cassidy, hid from the law in north-central Wyoming. Bounty hunters roamed the state, looking for outlaws. The modern ways that were changing life in many other states had yet to reach Wyoming.

Chinese coal miners being attacked in the Rock Springs Massacre of 1885

WORD TO KNOW

union *an organization formed by workers to try to improve working conditions and wages*

THE ROCK SPRINGS MASSACRE

One of the bleakest episodes in Wyoming history involved coal mining. Racial tensions and a labor dispute at the Rock Springs coal mine exploded into violence. On September 2, 1885, a mob of white coal miners and others attacked the town's Chinese neighborhood. They set fire to the homes of 79 Chinese people. Twenty-eight Chinese miners were killed, and as many as 22 others were injured in the turmoil. Survivors fled into the surrounding desert. One week later, federal troops escorted Chinese workers back to the mines. To maintain the uneasy peace, troops stayed in Rock Springs until 1898.

READ ABOUT

A train passes through Cheyenne in 1911.

▲**1925**
*Nellie Tayloe Ross
becomes the nation's
first female governor*

1950s
*Uranium deposits
are discovered in the
Powder River, Shirley,
and Wind River basins*

1957
*The legislature passes
the Wyoming Civil
Rights Act*

MORE MODERN TIMES

★

THE UNITED STATES' 1917 ENTRY INTO WORLD WAR I BROUGHT AN OIL BOOM AND MODERN TIMES TO WYOMING. The military needed oil to fuel warships, trucks, and tanks. Wartime demand led to an expansion of Wyoming's oil fields and an influx of workers. People in the state's oil towns had enough money to buy cars, radios, telephones, and tickets to motion picture shows.

1970s ►
Wyoming's population soars as the oil industry booms

1988
Fires destroy large swaths of Yellowstone National Park

2000s
Demand for Wyoming's coal supply grows

Albert Fall (far left) arrives at the Supreme Court with (left to right) oilman Edward Doheny and lawyers Frank Hogan and Mark Thompson in 1929.

THE TEAPOT DOME SCANDAL

In 1921, President Warren Harding ordered the Department of the Navy to transfer control of a Wyoming oil field to the U.S. Department of the Interior. The Teapot Dome oil field was named after a rock formation on the site that looked like a teapot. Secretary of the Interior Albert Fall leased the rights to drill in the Teapot Dome field to an oil-business friend. He did not ask other oil companies to bid for the drilling rights. Congress began investigating the Teapot Dome lease in 1922. They discovered that Fall had received cash and gifts in exchange for the lease. Seven years later, Fall was convicted of bribery and sentenced to a year in prison.

With newspaper headlines reporting the latest revelations, Teapot Dome quickly became the country's most powerful symbol of government corruption. Many voters switched their loyalties from the Republican Party to the Democrats. The Harding administration is remembered as one of the most corrupt in the nation's history.

DROUGHT AND DEPRESSION

Despite the wartime oil boom, little had changed for rural Wyomingites. The state sent 11,393 soldiers to fight in World War I. Most came home to the same Wyoming they had left. Few rural residents had electricity or other modern conveniences. A severe drought began in 1921. Along with falling prices for farm goods and livestock, the lack of water for crops and cattle eventually forced many farmers and ranchers to leave the state during the second half of the decade. Forty-two banks failed in Wyoming between 1921 and 1924.

By the early 1930s, Wyoming, like the other states, was in the grip of the Great Depression. Fifteen million of the country's 50 million workers were unemployed. Wyoming's oil towns were hit particularly hard. With so many people unemployed, few had enough money to buy gasoline and other petroleum products. Fuel prices fell. The state's largest employer, the Union Pacific Railroad, was also hit hard. With less freight

NELLIE TAYLOE ROSS: FIRST FEMALE GOVERNOR

Wyoming's Nellie Tayloe Ross (1876–1977) was the first woman governor in the United States. In October 1924, Ross's husband, Governor William Ross, died in office. In a special election held the next month, Wyoming voters elected Ross to finish her husband's term. She was inaugurated on January 5, 1925, and served until 1927. Ross ran for reelection in 1926 but lost. She later served as the director of the U.S. Mint.

? **Want to know more?** See http://wyoarchives.state.wy.us

A camp for the Civilian Conservation Corps, a New Deal program, in Bighorn National Forest

and fewer passengers to transport, the railroad laid off many workers in Wyoming. Prices for livestock and farm goods also plunged, leaving most of the state's ranchers and farmers poor.

In March 1933, President Franklin Roosevelt took office. He had the federal government create jobs for unemployed workers. They built hospitals, playgrounds, and dams to create electricity. Artists painted murals, writers wrote state histories, and photographers took pictures of people coping with the Depression. The Rural Electrification Administration brought electricity to thousands of Wyoming ranches and farms.

Not everyone in Wyoming welcomed Roosevelt's help, which was called the New Deal. Wyomingites had long prided themselves on their independence.

Many disliked the federal government. They bristled at any proposed federal meddling in their state's affairs. Even those who wanted federal help worried that the New Deal could harm Wyoming's traditional way of life. After New Deal successes were achieved in other states, much of this resistance weakened. Between 1933 and 1939, Wyoming received more federal money per person than any other state except Nevada. Federal soil conservation programs reversed the effects of the previous decade's drought, which had dried up much of the state's prime grazing lands.

The state legislature also took steps to improve the state's economy. The legislature rejected an income tax, but in 1935 it passed a law creating a state sales tax, meaning that people had to pay a tax on many items that they bought. The tax monies were used for state government projects and programs.

A NATION AT WAR

New Deal and local programs helped Wyomingites cope with the Great Depression, but the economy did not turn around until World War II (1939–1945). When the war began in Europe, people suddenly found work in coal mines and oil fields, which supplied fuel to U.S. allies. The state's oil and coal industries boomed again. In 1941, Japan attacked the American naval base at Pearl Harbor, Hawai'i, and the United States entered the war. The military needed oil to power airplanes, tanks, and other vehicles. Factories producing war goods needed coal to power their machinery.

Wyoming's oil and coal workers made an important contribution to the nation's war effort. Still other Wyomingites entered military service. More than 1,000 Wyoming troops lost their lives during the war.

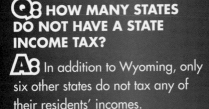

Q8 HOW MANY STATES DO NOT HAVE A STATE INCOME TAX?

A8 In addition to Wyoming, only six other states do not tax any of their residents' incomes.

The 3500th Flying Fortress, an airplane modified in Cheyenne for combat

WORDS TO KNOW

radioactive *giving off atomic particles, which can be dangerous to living things*

nuclear weapons *bombs or devices that use the energy created by splitting certain atoms (such as uranium) to create large explosions*

segregated *separated from others, according to race, class, ethnic group, religion, or other factors*

Q8 WHAT WAS THE SOVIET UNION?

A8 It was a large nation in eastern Europe and northern and central Asia. It formed in 1922 and broke apart into many different countries, including Russia, in 1991.

THE NUCLEAR AGE

In August 1945, the United States dropped two atomic bombs on Japan. The blasts and their **radioactive** dust killed as many as 200,000 people. Japan soon surrendered, ending the war in the Pacific.

By the early 1950s, distrust and competition between the United States and the Soviet Union grew into what was known as the cold war. Both sides built up their supply of **nuclear weapons**. The threat posed by these powerful weapons affected how the two countries and their allies acted toward one another. Ordinary Americans lived in fear of an atomic bomb being dropped on U.S. soil.

One key ingredient used to create the nuclear reaction in an atomic bomb was uranium. Uranium had first been discovered in Wyoming in 1918 near Lusk, in the eastern part of the state. In the early 1950s, large uranium deposits were found in the Powder River, Shirley, and Wind River basins. In these areas, a uranium boom lasted for several years. Warren Air Force Base near Cheyenne became a center for housing missiles that could reach the Soviet Union. These missiles were outfitted with nuclear warheads.

CIVIL RIGHTS

Although Wyoming calls itself the Equality State, it was one of the few states outside of the South in the 1950s that did not have a law banning **segregated** public accommodations. It had a small black population, only about 3,000, by 1950.

In 1954, two Wyoming men watched a restaurant manager refuse service to an African American soldier and his wife. The restaurant manager forced them to leave because of their race. The episode angered the two men, lawyer Teno Roncalio and physician Francis Barrett, who urged the state legislature to outlaw segregation. Roncalio had powerful friends in the state legislature, and Barrett's father was one of Wyoming's U.S. senators. After several failed bills, the Wyoming state legislature passed the 1957 Wyoming Civil Rights Act. This act outlawed racial discrimination in hotels, restaurants, and other public accommodations. Another equal rights law followed in 1964.

Members of the National Association of Colored Women meeting in Casper, 1953

MINI-BIO

TENO RONCALIO: POPULAR CONGRESSMAN

Born in Rock Springs, Teno Roncalio (1916–2003) was one of nine children in a coal miner's family. To pay for college, he worked at several jobs. He became a lawyer and was known for his efforts to enact the Wyoming Civil Rights Act. He then served as Wyoming's congressman in the U.S. House of Representatives for nine years (1965–1967 and 1971–1978). As a legislator, he worked to balance environmental preservation with economic development.

? **Want to know more?** See http://bioguide.congress.gov/scripts/biodisplay.pl?index=R000421

During the oil boom in the early 1970s, the population of Rock Springs doubled in two years!

A MODERN STATE

During the 1970s and 1980s, Wyoming's economy rose and fell, depending on the price of oil. In 1973, oil-producing nations in the Middle East refused to sell oil to the United States. This caused oil prices to soar in the United States. Higher prices convinced Wyoming's oil companies to pump more oil. They hired many new workers. Casper and other towns near oil fields boomed. Coal prices rose, too, and towns near coal mines, such as Rock Springs, Rawlins, and Gillette, grew rapidly. The state's population grew more than 40 percent between 1970 and 1980. Towns built new schools, roads, and housing developments.

Wyoming's energy boom lasted until 1982. By then, oil prices had dropped to half of the 1973 levels. When the oil, uranium, and coal-mining companies began to lay off workers, unemployment skyrocketed. Many people left the state to find jobs elsewhere. Wyoming's population dropped nearly 3 percent between 1980 and 1990. Once-thriving towns now had schools that were too big for their student bodies. Many of the houses built during the 1970s stood vacant.

By the 1960s, many Wyomingites saw the damage done by mining, livestock, and the military. They were convinced that Wyoming's land and natural resources should be protected. Others, however, felt that the state should encourage further industrial development to produce more jobs and revive the state's economy. In 1969, the state legislature passed a law that required companies to pay a tax for taking oil, coal, or minerals out of Wyoming. The state used the money to build schools, build and maintain highways, and fund other programs.

Concerns about the environment became stronger as tourism became more important to the state's

Hiking along Upper Green River Lake

economy. Wyoming's tourism industry started in 1872, when Yellowstone National Park became the world's first national park. In the 1960s, better highway systems increased tourism. The industry began to bring in lots of money and provided thousands of jobs. Like the oil and mining industries, Wyoming's tourism industry has experienced its ups and downs. In 1988, fires destroyed large swaths of Yellowstone National Park, and tourism dropped dramatically. Many hotel, restaurant, and tourism workers lost their jobs.

At the turn of the 21st century, Wyoming entered another boom cycle. New natural gas deposits were discovered near Pinedale. Demand for the state's coal and **coal bed methane** grew. By 2006, higher oil prices revitalized the state's oil industry. Northwestern Wyoming continued to benefit from tourism. As Wyomingites look toward the future, they hope that the state will be able to prosper while also protecting the environment that attracts so many people to it.

Wyoming collects about $50 million a year in taxes and royalties from the mining industry.

WORD TO KNOW

coal bed methane *a natural gas found in layers (beds) of coal*

READ ABOUT

A traditional
dancer at Wind
River Indian
Reservation

CHAPTER SIX

PEOPLE

★

WYOMING HAS THE SMALLEST POPULATION OF ANY STATE. About 65 percent of Wyoming residents make their homes in the state's larger towns. The other 35 percent live in small towns (less than 2,500 people) or rural areas. Wyoming's larger cities and small towns are spread out across the state. Wide stretches of nearly empty land often lie between towns. The state has only about 5 people per square mile (2 per sq km).

Downtown Jackson, which serves many tourists in the Jackson Hole resort region

SEE IT HERE!

SOUTH PASS CITY HISTORIC SITE

Wyoming has many ghost towns, settlements that once thrived but are now abandoned. Many of them enjoyed a brief boom because of the discovery of coal, oil, or gold or because railroads were being built. When gold was discovered near South Pass City in 1867, its population quickly swelled to more than 2,000 people. Prospectors soon mined most of the gold and moved on. Today, South Pass City has been restored. Visitors can explore 25 homes and shops, a theater, a hotel, and saloons to get a glimpse of the town's boomtown days.

URBAN CENTERS

Cheyenne, the capital city, and Casper, an oil center, are Wyoming's only cities with populations greater than 50,000. Wyoming's other "big cities" are not very big. Only Laramie and Gillette have more than 20,000 people. Laramie is the home of the University of Wyoming, and Gillette is a coal mining and oil center. Other important towns are regional hubs of mining, agriculture, or tourism. These include Rock Springs, Evanston, Green River, Sheridan, and Jackson.

Where Wyomingites Live

The colors on this map indicate population density throughout the state. The darker the color, the more people live there.

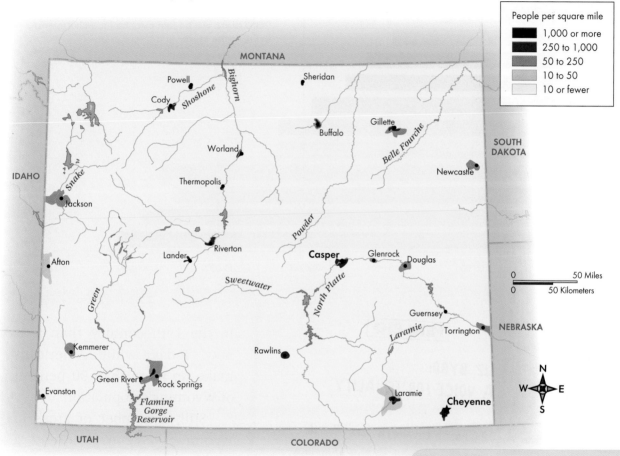

People per square mile

- ■ 1,000 or more
- ■ 250 to 1,000
- ■ 50 to 250
- ■ 10 to 50
- □ 10 or fewer

GROWING DIVERSITY

Wyoming coal miners in the 19th century were from a wide variety of ethnic groups. Rock Springs was one of the most ethnically diverse towns in America in the 1880s. It was home to Italians, Chinese, Greeks, Finns, Irish, African Americans, Czechs, and people from many other groups. Wyoming was actually more diverse

Big City Life

This list shows the population of Wyoming's biggest cities.

Cheyenne	55,731
Casper	51,738
Laramie	26,050
Gillette	22,685
Rock Springs	18,772

Source: U.S. Census Bureau, 2005 estimate

Wyoming Population Growth

This chart shows Wyoming's population changes between 1870 and 2000, and it projects that by 2010 there will be just over half a million people living in the state.

Source: U.S. Census Bureau

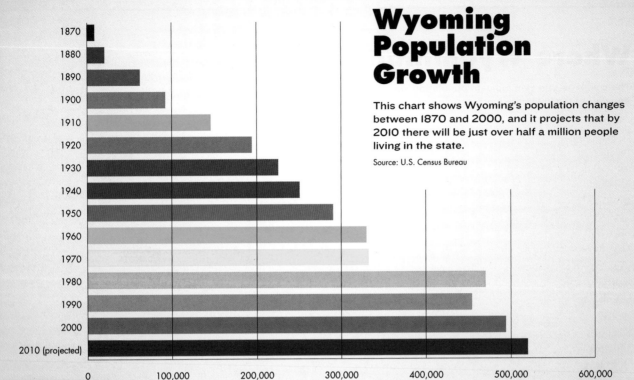

MINI-BIO

LIZ BYRD: A VOICE FOR EQUALITY

Harriett Elizabeth "Liz" Byrd (1926–) served in the Wyoming Legislature for 12 years (1981–1993). Born and raised in Cheyenne, she worked as an elementary school teacher for nearly 40 years. As a legislator representing Laramie County, she supported laws raising pay for teachers, improving child safety, and establishing Equality Day in Wyoming. She was the first African American woman to serve in the Wyoming Legislature.

? **Want to know more?** See www.madeinwyoming.net/profiles/byrd.php

in the 19th century than it is now. Today, white Americans make up more than 90 percent of Wyoming's population.

Still, a number of areas in Wyoming have experienced a sizable increase in Hispanic residents over the past two decades. Hispanics make up more than 10 percent of the population in Carbon, Washakie, Laramie, Sweetwater, and Teton counties. Teton County has one of the fastest-growing Mexican communities in the country. Only 1 percent of county residents were Hispanic in 1990. Today, Hispanics make up about 20 percent of Teton County's population. Jobs in the county's large tourism industry have attracted many of these new residents.

Native Americans make up approximately 2.5 percent of the state's population. Most are members of the Shoshone and Arapaho nations. The 2.2-million-acre (890,000 ha) Wind River Indian Reservation, shared by Shoshones and Arapahos, puts the Native American population of Fremont County at more than 20 percent.

DANELLE MOYTE: HONORING TRADITIONS

Danelle Moyte (1986–) is the director of Las Flores de Colores, a dance troupe that performs traditional Mexican dances. She started the troupe in 2002, when she was still a student at Cheyenne's Central High School. She now supervises the dancers, teaching them teamwork and dances from various regions of Mexico. Las Flores de Colores performs at schools, festivals, and other occasions.

Want to know more? See www.lasfloresdecolores.com

People QuickFacts

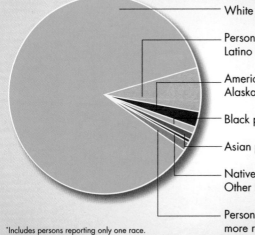

White persons not Hispanic: 87.3%

Persons of Hispanic or Latino origin: 7.4%†

American Indian and Alaska Native persons: 2.5%*

Black persons: 1.2%*

Asian persons: 0.7%*

Native Hawaiian and Other Pacific Islanders: 0.1%*

Persons reporting two or more races: 1.4%

*Includes persons reporting only one race.
†Hispanics may be of any race, so they are also included in applicable race categories.

Between 2006 and 2007, Wyoming's immigrant population soared by 17.5 percent, the largest percentage gain in the country. More than half of the new residents were from Latin America, primarily Mexico.

HOW TO TALK LIKE A WYOMINGITE

If you want to talk like a Wyomingite, you might need to learn some cowboy and rodeo words. After saddling up your bangtail (horse), follow the trail boss (the leader of a cattle drive). Because you're a tenderfoot (inexperienced cowboy or cowgirl), be careful not to bite the dust (get thrown off your horse). Keep your eyes peeled for barking squirrels (prairie dogs). If you see a gullywasher (heavy rainstorm) approaching, you may want to head back to the barn. On Saturday, head into Rodeo Town (Cheyenne) for some big-city fun.

HOW TO EAT LIKE A WYOMINGITE

Many favorite Wyoming foods come from cowboy days. Cowboys often had to carry their own food or cook what they could find out on the range. Dried beans and dried meat were popular because they were filling and didn't weigh much. The state's two major livestock animals—cows and sheep—influence Wyoming cooking. Beef and lamb dishes often appear on Wyoming dinner tables.

The dining area of the Old Faithful Inn, Yellowstone National Park

MENU

WHAT'S ON THE MENU IN WYOMING?

★ ★ ★

Pinto beans

Pinto Beans

Pinto beans are a type of dried bean that have distinctive spots that look like those on a pinto, a spotted horse. Most types turn pink when cooked, and they're a good source of protein.

Beef Jerky

Jerky is strips of meat that are preserved by drying and salting. Beef jerky and other types of jerky make good travel foods because they don't need refrigeration.

Lamb Stew

Lamb stew is made by slowly cooking chunks of lamb meat and vegetables in water. Popular vegetables for lamb stew include potatoes, carrots, beans, and tomatoes.

Rocky Mountain Trout

Wyoming's Rocky Mountain streams are chock-full of trout. One popular trout recipe is to lightly coat the fish fillets (long slices of boneless fish meat) with flour and fry them in a pan.

Chokecherry Pudding

This Native American dessert combines chokecherries with sugar, flour, and water. A chokecherry is a small, dark-colored fruit similar to the black cherry.

Lamb stew

TRY THIS RECIPE
Wyoming Chili

For a taste of cowboy cooking, prepare a big pot of chili. There are as many chili recipes in Wyoming as there are cooks. Here's one version. Have an adult nearby to help.

Ingredients:
2 tablespoons oil
6 garlic cloves, diced
2 onions, diced
1½ pounds ground beef or lamb (omit for vegetarian chili)
1 14.5-ounce can diced tomatoes, drained
2 tablespoons chili powder
1 teaspoon cumin
Salt and pepper to taste
1 14.5-ounce can red kidney beans, drained
4 ounces grated cheddar cheese

Instructions:
1. Heat the oil in a large, heavy saucepan.
2. Cook the garlic and onion in the oil over medium heat for 5 minutes.
3. Add the meat. Stir frequently and cook until browned, about 10 minutes.
4. Add the tomatoes and spices. Stir well to combine.
5. Cover and simmer on low for 45 minutes, stirring occasionally.
6. Add the beans and simmer for 15 minutes, stirring occasionally.
7. Ladle into serving bowls and top with grated cheese. Makes 4 servings.

Older students helping kindergartners with their computer skills at a school on the Wind River Indian Reservation

SCHOOL DAYS

Education is a leading concern of people in Wyoming. Wyoming is one of the top states in the amount of money spent per student, thanks largely to tax revenues from mining, oil, and gas production.

The University of Wyoming is the state's only four-year public college. It is a major research university, known for its work in agriculture, energy, and natural resources. More than 13,000 students take courses on its campus in Laramie. It also offers classes or services in all of Wyoming's 23 counties. Seven community colleges provide educational opportunities on campuses around the state. These colleges award two-year degrees and provide career training and other educational programs.

LITERATURE

Wyoming's scenic beauty and deserted open spaces have provided dramatic settings for many authors. The book that most people associate with Wyoming is Owen Wister's *The Virginian* (1902). The novel's unnamed hero, the Virginian, battles a bad guy named Trampas. *The Virginian*'s portrayal of cowboy life in Wyoming and its duel between the two main characters provided a model for many Western novels and movies. One of these later Western novels is Jack Schaefer's *Shane* (1954). It is based on the Johnson County War of 1892. Mary O'Hara wrote several popular novels while living on a ranch in Laramie County. Her best-known works are *My Friend Flicka* (1941), about a 10-year-old boy and his horse, and *Green Grass of Wyoming* (1946).

Pulitzer Prize–winner Annie Proulx explores Western themes in her novels and short stories. She was born and raised on the East Coast, but one of her ancestors was a fur trapper in Wyoming in the 1820s. All of the stories in her short story collection *Close Range: Wyoming Stories* (1999) are set in rural Wyoming, where she now lives.

Celebrated writer Ernest Hemingway spent time fishing and hunting near Yellowstone National Park. He wrote two nonfiction books, *Death in the Afternoon*

Pulitzer Prize–winning writer Annie Proulx was born in Connecticut but makes her home in Wyoming.

JACKSON POLLOCK: ABSTRACT PAINTER

Jackson Pollock (1912—1956) was a leading abstract artist known for his wild, energetic, and colorful paintings. Born in Cody, Wyoming, Pollock grew up in Arizona and California. He moved to New York in 1930 to study art. He was a member of a group of artists known as abstract expressionists. Rather than using paintbrushes, they smeared, dribbled, splashed, and poured paint onto canvases.

? Want to know more? See www.nga.gov/feature/pollock/pollockhome.shtm

(1932) and *Green Hills of Africa* (1935), and his novel *To Have and Have Not* while staying in Wyoming. Contemporary writers living in Wyoming include Gretel Ehrlich, Mark Spragg, Michael and Kathleen Gear, Jeffe Kennedy, and Gerry Spence.

Wyoming is home to several noted authors of books for young readers. Will Hobbs has written more than a dozen outdoor adventure novels, including *Downriver* (1995) and *Far North* (1996). His *Ghost Canoe* received the Edgar Allan Poe Award for best young-adult mystery in 1998. Cheyenne-born Patricia MacLachlan won the Newbery Medal in 1986 for her novel *Sarah, Plain and Tall*.

MUSIC

Classical music fans enjoy performances by Casper's Wyoming Symphony Orchestra and the Cheyenne Symphony Orchestra. Annual music festivals held in Wyoming include the Grand Teton Music Festival and the Bluegrass Festival in Jackson Hole, and the Old-time Fiddlers' Contest, held in different locations.

Laramie-born Mike Hurwitz used his experiences as a cowboy, bronco buster, and hunting guide to create his own style of country blues and cowboy music. He lives in Alta and performs all over the United States. Another singing cowboy, rodeo star Chris LeDoux, made such hit albums as *Whatcha Gonna Do with a Cowboy* (1992).

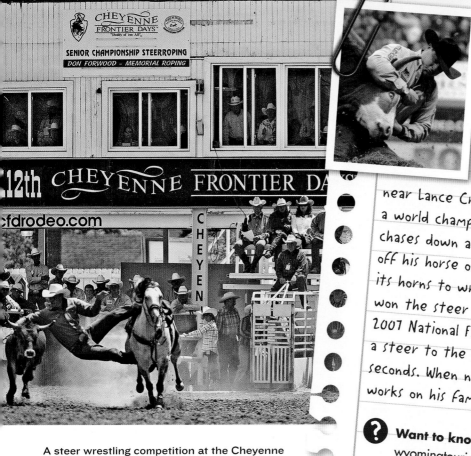

A steer wrestling competition at the Cheyenne Frontier Days Rodeo

MINI-BIO

JASON MILLER: STEER WRESTLER

Born and raised on a ranch near Lance Creek, Jason Miller (1974–) is a world champion steer wrestler. Miller chases down a steer on horseback, jumps off his horse onto the steer, and twists its horns to wrestle it to the ground. He won the steer wrestling event at the 2007 National Finals Rodeo by wrestling a steer to the ground in an amazing 4.8 seconds. When not competing in rodeos, he works on his family's cattle ranch.

? **Want to know more?** See www.wyomingtourism.org/cms/d/jason_miller.php

SPORTS

Rodeo is one of the biggest sports in Wyoming. Joe Alexander, Brandie Halls, Jim Houston, Jason Miller, and Bill Smith are just a few of Wyoming's rodeo stars of the past and present. Cheyenne Frontier Days attracts more than 300,000 people to the capital city in July for a world-class rodeo and other Western activities. Popular rodeo competitions are bareback bronc riding, steer wrestling, tie-down roping, and barrel racing, in which horse and rider try to gallop around a pattern of barrels without knocking any over.

Many Wyomingites are proud and passionate fans of the University of Wyoming's sports teams. They cheer the Cowboys and Cowgirls as they compete in football, basketball, and other sports.

Ken Sailors of Laramie invented the basketball jump shot in the yard of his family farm near Hillsdale, Wyoming, when he was a boy. He used the shot to help the University of Wyoming basketball team win the NCAA tournament in 1943.

READ ABOUT

A group of people assembled at the site of the Wyoming Constitutional Convention of 1889

CHAPTER SEVEN

GOVERNMENT

★

IN SEPTEMBER OF 1889, DELEGATES FROM WYOMING TERRITORY MET IN CHEYENNE TO DRAFT A STATE CONSTITUTION. Forty-five delegates signed the constitution with a pen made out of Wyoming gold. Voters approved the constitution on November 5, 1889. When Congress admitted Wyoming into the Union the following year, the constitution became the supreme law of the new state. The Wyoming Constitution has 21 sections that guarantee the rights of the state's citizens, provide a framework for the state's government, and outline the law on many issues.

The state capitol in Cheyenne

Capitol Facts

Here are some fascinating facts about Wyoming's state capitol.

Exterior height: 146 feet (45 m)
Number of stories high: 3½ (plus dome)
Length: 300 feet (91 m)
Width: 112 feet (34 m)
Dome: 50-foot (15 m) diameter at base
Construction dates: 1887–1890; 1917
Cost of construction: $150,000
Cost of 1980 renovation: $7.6 million
Notable artworks: Murals in the house and senate chambers by Allen T. True (designer of the bucking bronco on Wyoming license plates); stained-glass state seal on each chamber's ceiling

WYOMING'S STATE CAPITOL

Wyoming's capitol is located in downtown Cheyenne. It was designed to resemble the U.S. Capitol in Washington, D.C. Workers used gray sandstone from quarries near Rawlins to make the upper floors. The dome is covered with a thin sheet of gold. When it opened in 1890, the capitol featured the newest conveniences: running water, natural gas, and electricity. Two wings were added in 1917 for the senate and house chambers.

Capital City

This map shows places of interest in Cheyenne, Wyoming's capital city.

THE LEGISLATIVE BRANCH

The Wyoming state legislature's job is to make new laws and change or get rid of old laws. It also recommends changes to the state's constitution. Unlike those in some other states, Wyoming's 30 senators and 60 representatives are not full-time legislators. They don't have offices in the capitol, and they work at their regular jobs when the legislature is not in session. Ranchers, farmers, railroad workers, teachers, and people in many other professions represent their fellow citizens in the legislature. Senators can serve no more than three four-year terms during a 24-year period. Representatives can serve no more than six two-year terms during a 24-year period.

FRANCIS E. WARREN: GOVERNOR AND U.S. SENATOR

Born in Massachusetts, Francis E. Warren (1844–1929) moved to Wyoming in 1868. The successful businessman became active in the territory's politics, serving as governor of Wyoming Territory. In 1890, he was elected as the state's first governor and soon resigned to serve as one of the state's first U.S. senators. Known for his work on land, forestry, and military legislation, Warren served in the Senate until his death.

? Want to know more? See http://wyoarchives.state.wy.us

Wyoming's first governor, Francis E. Warren, served for less than 50 days. Six weeks after voters elected him governor, the state legislature elected him to be the state's first U.S. senator. He decided to take the Senate seat.

The state legislature holds law-making sessions in odd-numbered years only. In even-numbered years, the legislature meets to settle on the state's budget. Together, the lawmaking and budget sessions can last no more than 60 working days during a two-year period. The state constitution does allow the governor or the state legislature to call special legislative or budget sessions.

THE EXECUTIVE BRANCH

The governor is the head of the executive branch of Wyoming's government. Voters elect the governor to serve a four-year term. A governor can serve no more than eight years in a 16-year period. The governor is responsible for making sure that state laws are carried out. He or she may suggest new laws to the legislature. The governor approves the laws passed by the legislature by signing each bill. The governor has the power to veto, or reject, these bills. The legislature, however, can override a veto with a two-thirds vote. The law will then go into effect despite the governor's veto.

The governor appoints other state officials to oversee various departments. These departments include Agriculture, Game and Fish, Travel and Tourism, Livestock Board, Transportation, and Environmental Quality. The governor also appoints judges to the state supreme court.

Wyoming state senator Jayne Mockler talks to a colleague during a budget discussion at the capitol.

MINI-BIO

DAVID FREUDENTHAL: POPULAR GOVERNOR

David Freudenthal (1950–) was born in Thermopolis and grew up in a large farming family. After college, Freudenthal worked as an economist for the State of Wyoming and attended law school. He opened his own law office in 1980 and was appointed U.S. attorney for Wyoming in 1994. In 2002, he was elected governor in a close race. In 2006, the popular governor was reelected in a landslide. As governor, he has tried to strike a balance between industrial development and environmental protection.

? **Want to know more?** See http://governor. wy.gov/first-family/dave-bio.html

In addition to the governor, voters elect four officials in the executive branch. They are secretary of state (who handles state elections, various services to businesses, and other administrative services), auditor (who reviews the state's financial records), treasurer (who manages the state's money), and superintendent of public education (who oversees the state's school system). If the governor cannot complete his or her term, the secretary of state takes over until the next election.

SEE IT HERE!

THE GOVERNOR'S MANSION

Wyoming's governor's mansion is located in the northwestern corner of Cheyenne. It has served as the governor's home since 1976. The grand house is made of redwood boards and rocks from quarries northeast of Cheyenne. The original residence, the Historic Governors' Mansion, is a modest red-brick house built in 1905. It has been a museum since 1977.

Wyoming State Government

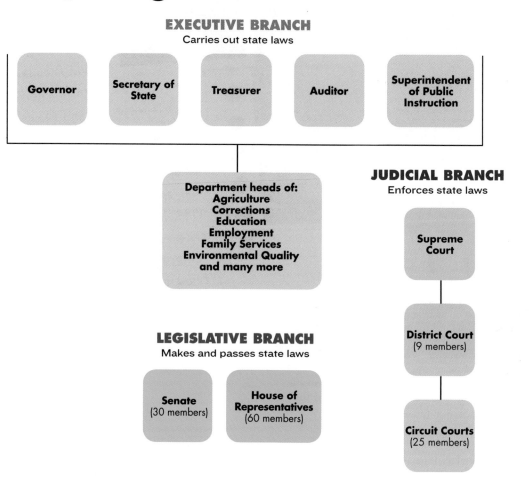

EXECUTIVE BRANCH
Carries out state laws

| Governor | Secretary of State | Treasurer | Auditor | Superintendent of Public Instruction |

Department heads of:
**Agriculture
Corrections
Education
Employment
Family Services
Environmental Quality
and many more**

JUDICIAL BRANCH
Enforces state laws

Supreme Court

District Court
(9 members)

Circuit Courts
(25 members)

LEGISLATIVE BRANCH
Makes and passes state laws

Senate
(30 members)

House of Representatives
(60 members)

Representing Wyoming

This list shows the number of elected officials who represent Wyoming, both on the state and national levels.

OFFICE	NUMBER	LENGTH OF TERM
State senators	30	4 years
State representatives	60	2 years
U.S. senators	2	6 years
U.S. representatives	1	2 years
Presidential electors	3	—

THE JUDICIAL BRANCH

The Wyoming Supreme Court is the state's highest court. Its five justices serve eight-year terms. The governor appoints the justices, but in the next scheduled statewide election after a justice is appointed, voters decide whether that justice keeps his or her position. The Wyoming Supreme Court hears appeals of decisions made by lower courts.

Wyoming has nine district courts, which have a total of 21 judges. These courts hear major criminal cases, involving crimes such as robbery or assault, and civil cases, such as disputes over property or personal injury cases. District courts also handle all cases involving juveniles. District court judges serve six-year terms. They are appointed by the governor and must be approved by voters in the next election.

District courts also hear appeals of circuit court decisions. Wyoming's circuit courts handle misdemeanor (minor) criminal cases and minor lawsuits between people. The governor appoints the 25 circuit court judges, and voters decide whether each judge keeps his or her position.

In the juvenile justice system, lawbreakers usually either receive a warning for their first offense or face a trial in juvenile court. With the support of educators and lawyers, four Wyoming cities have created alternative youth courts. Municipal court judges or justices of the peace supervise the courts, and teenagers run them. Teens serve as the court's judge, lawyers, and jury members.

MINI-BIO

WILLIS VAN DEVANTER: SUPREME COURT JUSTICE

Willis Van Devanter (1859–1941) served on the U.S. Supreme Court for 26 years (1911–1937). Born in Indiana, he moved to Cheyenne in 1884. He opened a law practice and served as a member of the territorial government and on the territory's supreme court. President Theodore Roosevelt appointed Van Devanter to the U.S. Court of Appeals in 1903. Seven years later, President William Taft appointed him to the U.S. Supreme Court. Van Devanter was known for his opposition to many New Deal programs and his expertise on little-known federal laws.

? Want to know more? See www.supremecourthistory.org/02_history/subs_timeline/images_associates/053.html

FAQ

Q8 HOW DID CIRCUIT COURTS GET THEIR NAME?

A8 In the old days, judges traveled around a large area, making a circuit (circle), to hold trials in different towns. Today, there are many more judges and courts, so judges don't have to travel.

The court cannot sentence a defendant to imprisonment, but it can charge minor fines. The court can also impose alternative sentences, such as repairing damaged property, performing community service, or serving on the youth court.

LOCAL RULE

Wyoming's county and city governments do many things, from collecting taxes and keeping property records to maintaining roads and providing law enforcement. Voters elect county commissioners to over-

Residents prepare to vote in an election in Casper.

WACKY LAWS

Wyoming has some pretty wacky laws. Though the laws below are not enforced, they are still on the books:

- It is illegal to take a picture of a rabbit from January to April without an official permit.
- It is illegal to wear a hat that obstructs people's view in a theater.

Wyoming Counties

This map shows the 23 counties in Wyoming. Cheyenne, the state capital, is indicated with a star.

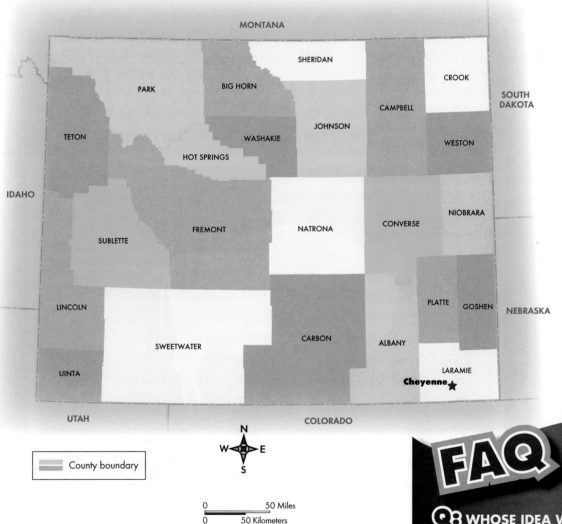

MONTANA

SHERIDAN

CROOK

PARK

BIG HORN

CAMPBELL

SOUTH DAKOTA

JOHNSON

TETON

WASHAKIE

WESTON

HOT SPRINGS

IDAHO

NIOBRARA

FREMONT

NATRONA

CONVERSE

SUBLETTE

PLATTE

GOSHEN

NEBRASKA

LINCOLN

CARBON

ALBANY

SWEETWATER

LARAMIE

UINTA

Cheyenne ★

UTAH

COLORADO

▨ County boundary

N
W ✦ E
S

0   50 Miles
0   50 Kilometers

see their county government. Each county has a clerk, treasurer, assessor, sheriff, and various other officials. Wyoming's cities and towns elect mayors and councils to manage local affairs.

FAQ

Q8 WHOSE IDEA WAS IT TO HAVE YOUTH COURTS IN WYOMING?

A8 Teens attending a youth summit in 1995 asked the state to create youth courts. The next year, the Wyoming State Legislature made them legal.

State Flag

Wyoming's state flag was adopted in 1917. It consists of a white bison facing left on a rectangular blue field (background). A thin white border and a wider red border surround the field. The flag uses the three colors of the American flag. The bison is Wyoming's state mammal and an enduring symbol of the Great Plains. The state seal is emblazoned on the bison.

State Seal

The Great Seal of Wyoming depicts a female statue standing in front of a banner that reads "Equal Rights." The banner pays tribute to Wyoming being the first state to give women the right to vote and hold public office. Two pillars on each side of the statue hold up burning lamps, which represent the light of knowledge. Scrolls in front of the pillars point out Wyoming's four major economic strengths: livestock, grain, mines, and oil. Below the statue, an eagle holds a shield with stripes and a star, representing Wyoming's dedication to the Union. The number 44 in the star identifies Wyoming as the 44th state. The two dates beside the shield give the years that Wyoming became a territory (1869) and a state (1890). Two male figures stand beside the pillars. The cowboy represents the cattle-ranching industry, and the miner represents the mining industry. The seal's outer border reads "Great Seal of the State of Wyoming."

98

READ ABOUT

Harvesting wheat
near Cheyenne

ECONOMY

★

WYOMING'S HUGE MOUNTAINS AND VAST PLAINS STAND ON LARGE OIL AND NATURAL GAS RESERVES AND RICH DEPOSITS OF COAL AND OTHER MINERALS. The state has excellent grazing lands for cattle and sheep, and its spectacular scenery draws tourists from around the world. Despite all of these riches, Wyoming still has the third-smallest state economy in the United States. The state has a small population and no large cities. More than 90 percent of its land is rural. It has fewer manufacturing industries than most other states.

CHAPTER EIGHT

Ranchers carry sheep to be sheared near Buffalo.

The average size of a Wyoming farm or ranch is 3,651 acres (1,478 ha). The average size of all farms and ranches in the United States is only 444 acres (180 ha).

AGRICULTURE

Agriculture represents less than 3 percent of employment in the state. More than 17,000 people work on farms and ranches or have related jobs, such as processing or transporting agricultural products. More than 34.4 million acres (13.9 million ha) in Wyoming are devoted to 8,800 operating farms and ranches. Wyoming's agricultural sector is worth about $1 billion a year.

The cattle industry is the state's largest agricultural segment. Wyoming has more than 1.5 million cows. Because grass does not grow plentifully in the state, ranchers need large grazing lands to feed their cattle.

Major Agricultural and Mining Products

This map shows where Wyoming's major agricultural and mining products come from. See a cow? That means cattle are raised there.

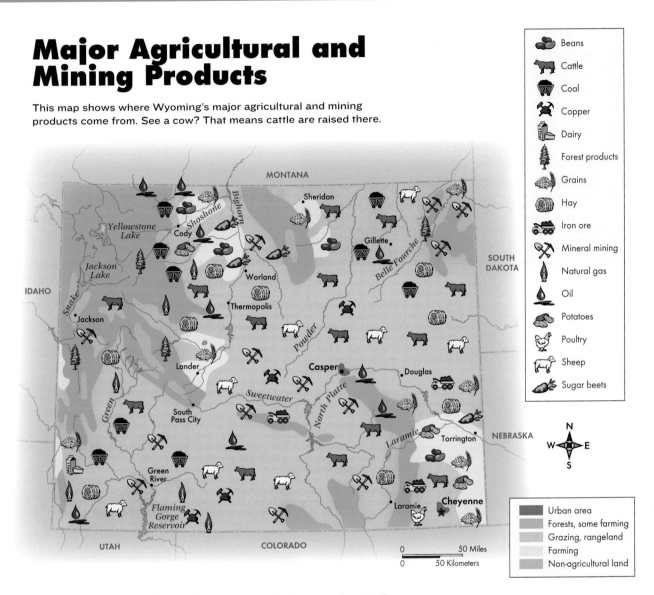

Beans	
Cattle	
Coal	
Copper	
Dairy	
Forest products	
Grains	
Hay	
Iron ore	
Mineral mining	
Natural gas	
Oil	
Potatoes	
Poultry	
Sheep	
Sugar beets	

Urban area	
Forests, some farming	
Grazing, rangeland	
Farming	
Non-agricultural land	

Sheep graze in places that are unfit for cattle. Today, the state has more than 450,000 sheep and lambs. It ranks third among the states in the number of sheep and lambs and second in wool production.

Although not directly important to the economy, horses are essential in cattle ranching. Ranchers and cowboys prize their horses, carefully training them to work on the ranch.

Wyoming's Brand Book lists more than 28,000 cattle brands.

SADDLE MAKER

Don King (1923–2007) was a celebrated Western saddle maker. Born in Douglas, King learned to make leather goods as a teenager. He worked on ranches and in saddle shops in several other states before settling in Sheridan at age 23. He ran his own 200-acre (81 ha) ranch. A local saddle maker taught him how to make saddles, and in 1957, he began making saddles full-time. He is known for his trophy saddles, which are presented as prizes at rodeos.

The state's major crops are hay, sugar beets, barley, corn, wheat, oats, dry beans, and alfalfa. Hay, wheat, and barley grow well in dry areas. Irrigation makes growing other crops such as beets and beans possible.

ENERGY AND MINING

Energy and mining products make up the largest industrial sector of Wyoming's economy. Major energy and mining products in the state are crude oil, coal, natural gas, coal bed methane, trona, and other minerals. These products generate about one-fourth of the total value of all the goods and services produced in the state.

A worker checks a reading at a Wyoming oil refinery.

Should Drilling on Federal Lands Be Expanded?

PRO

One way to make the United States less dependent on energy supplies from other countries is to increase oil and natural gas production in this country. Rich oil and natural gas deposits lie underneath many federal lands in Wyoming and other states. The American Petroleum Institute emphasizes, "Greater access to these areas is needed because that's where the remaining oil and natural gas accumulations are likely to be located—particularly the larger ones." New drilling operations will provide jobs. Increased production of oil and natural gas will lower fuel prices for consumers.

CON

The Wilderness Society president William Meadows argues, "Instead of promoting policies . . . that will encourage more [public] lands to be open for energy development . . . our real priority should be to make sure that we do not sacrifice in the long term our last remaining wild places." The best way to make the United States less dependent on foreign energy supplies is to conserve fuels. The Natural Resources Defense Council stresses, "A faster, cleaner and cheaper path to energy security is to reduce demand for oil."

Oil has been found in all but one of the state's counties. Wyoming oil wells yield about 55 million barrels of oil each year. Crude oil is used to make gasoline, paint, plastics, and other goods. Although many of its oil fields have been used up, Wyoming still ranks seventh nationwide in oil production.

Wyoming produces about 430 million tons of coal each year. It is the number-one producer of coal in the United States, providing 38 percent of coal produced in the nation. The nation's 10 top-producing mines are located in Wyoming, and the world's largest surface coal-mining operation is located near Gillette.

LOW SULFUR COAL

Coal is made up of many different chemicals, including sulfur. When power plants and factories burn coal, sulfur is released into the atmosphere. Sulfur particles combine with moisture in the air to produce sulfuric acid. This harmful chemical is one of the causes of acid rain, which damages forests and other plant life. Wyoming coal is valuable because it has an extremely low amount of sulfur. Its sulfur content is about 0.5 percent. Coal from the eastern United States has a sulfur content of 3 percent or higher.

A coal mine near Gillette

Q8 WHAT IS NATURAL GAS?

A8 It's a colorless gas that is found underneath the earth's surface. It burns easily and is used for heating, cooking, and other purposes.

Scientists estimate that Wyoming has more than 1.4 trillion tons of coal. That's the largest coal reserve in the country. About 90 percent of the state's coal mines are located in the northeast corner of the state.

Wyoming ranks first in mining employment in the United States. Coal-mining companies employ more than 6,000 Wyomingites. An additional 18,000 Wyoming workers have jobs related to coal. Wages in the coal-mining industry are twice the state average of $33,000. Coal mining is one of the most dangerous jobs in the world. But surface mining, as practiced in Wyoming, is much safer than the underground coal mining done in many other states.

Wyoming ranks second in the nation in natural gas production. It produces more than 18 trillion cubic feet (500 billion cubic meters) of natural gas. Natural gas is used mostly for heating homes and businesses. Another important gas produced in Wyoming is coal bed methane. It's a type of natural gas extracted from coal bed seams. The coal fields in the Powder River Basin produce much of the state's coal bed methane.

Wyoming has the largest known reserve of trona in the world. What is trona? It is a mineral that is a source for sodium carbonate. Sodium carbonate is used to make glass, paper, soap, medicines, mold killers, toothpaste, swimming pool chemicals, water softeners, and many other goods. The state produces more than 17 million tons of trona each year. Wyoming is the nation's leading producer of uranium, a metal used today mostly as a fuel in nuclear power plants. Wyoming mines also produce gold, iron, and various clays. Many gemstones are mined in the state, including jade, rubies, jasper, and even diamonds.

SERVICE INDUSTRIES

Service industries make up about 60 percent of the value of Wyoming's economy. Store clerks, teachers, bankers, doctors, and real estate agents are among the many types of service industry workers.

Top Products

Agriculture Cattle and sheep, hay, barley, beans, wheat, sugar beets
Manufacturing Petroleum and coal products, nonelectric machinery, stone, clay and glass products, printing and publishing, food products, lumber and wood products
Mining Coal, oil, natural gas, uranium, sodium carbonate, stone, jade, rubies, jasper, diamonds

WORD TO KNOW

dry goods *clothing, cloth, and related goods*

MINI-BIO

J. C. PENNEY: RETAIL PIONEER

James Cash Penney (1875–1971) built a large, successful department store chain. The 24-year-old Missourian was sent to manage a Denver-based dry goods store. In 1902, Penney opened his own dry goods store in Kemmerer. By 1913, he had opened up 33 more J.C. Penney stores. Over the years, the chain grew. Penney began selling a wider range of merchandise in his stores. At his death, there were 1,660 J. C. Penney department stores in North America.

Want to know more? See http://shs.umsystem.edu/famousmissourians/entrepreneurs/penney/penney.shtml

The federal government employs more workers than any other employer in Wyoming. The United States owns about half of the state's land. Many federal workers in Wyoming manage these lands. They control logging and grazing rights on federal lands. They maintain the national forests, national monuments, and national parks in the state.

What Do Wyomingites Do?

This color-coded chart shows what industries Wyomingites work in.

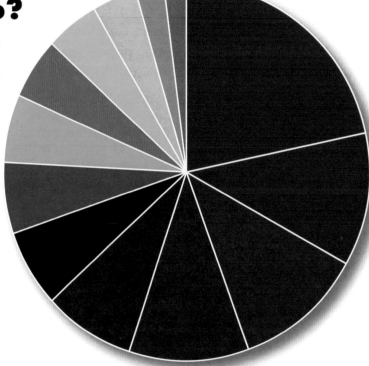

21.7%	Educational services, health care, and social assistance, 59,137
11.5%	Retail trade, 31,508
11.4%	Agriculture, forestry, fishing, hunting, and mining, 31,011
10.5%	Arts, entertainment, recreation, accommodation, and food services, 28,489

8.1%	Construction, 22,039
6.6%	Transportation, warehousing, and utilities, 18,104
6.2%	Professional, scientific, management, administrative, and waste management services, 17,011
5.9%	Public administration, 16,105

5.2%	Manufacturing, 14,119
4.6%	Other services, except public administration, 12,535
4.1%	Finance, insurance, real estate, rental, and leasing, 11,185
2.5%	Wholesale trade, 6,874
1.7%	Information, 4,551

Source: U.S. Census Bureau, 2006 estimate

A family checks a map at Yellowstone National Park.

TOURISM

The tourism and recreation industry is the state's second-largest industry. It accounts for more than $1 billion in annual revenue. Wyoming's tourism industry employs more than 37,000 people, either full- or part-time. With its ski resorts, national parks, and 10 million acres (4 million ha) of forested land, Wyoming boasts many recreational opportunities. State and national parks and monuments alone attract more than 7 million visitors each year, including hunters and fishers. Wyoming's Wild West heritage lives on in rodeos, roundups, dude ranches, and frontier festivals throughout the state.

Wyoming's Biggest Attractions

Approximate number of visitors in 2008:

Yellowstone National Park: 3.1 million
Grand Teton National Park: 2.5 million
Cheyenne Frontier Days: 525,000
Devils Tower National Monument: 335,000

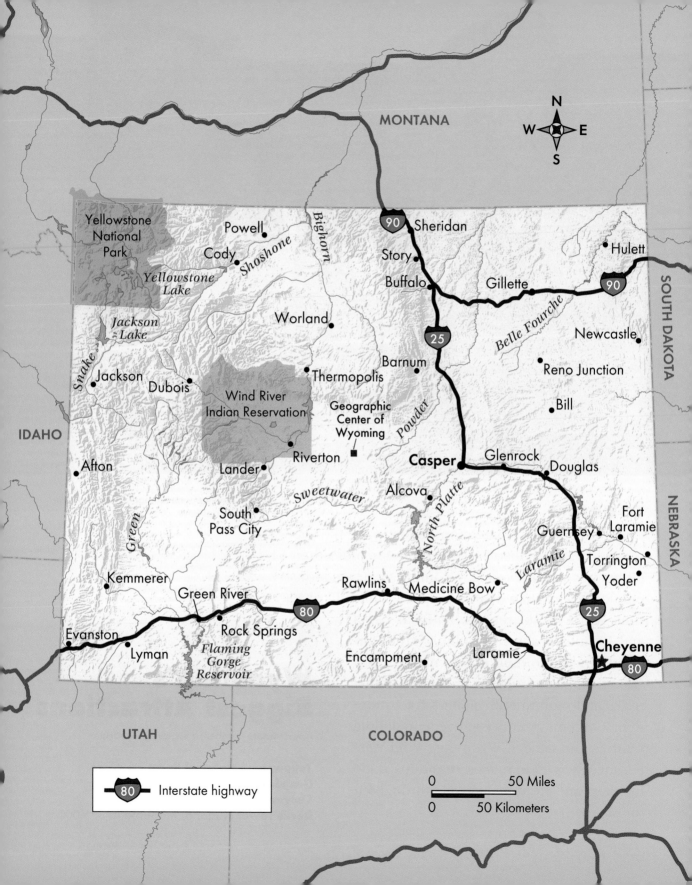

CHAPTER NINE

TRAVEL GUIDE

★

RUGGED MOUNTAINS. Dry deserts. Wide open spaces. Get out there and enjoy Wyoming's natural beauty! See bears, elk, and other wildlife at Yellowstone National Park. From Afton to Yoder, Wyoming's small towns also have lots to offer. And don't forget the cities. Check out the Buffalo Bill Historical Center in Cody, and enjoy the festivities at Cheyenne Frontier Days. There's a lot to do in Wyoming, so let's get going.

← Follow along with this travel map. We'll start in Jackson and end our trip in Lyman.

NORTHWEST

THINGS TO DO: Swoosh down the ski slopes, watch Old Faithful erupt, and take a dip in some hot springs.

Jackson

★ **Yellowstone National Park:** Most visitors to this park hope to get a glimpse of Old Faithful spouting, but there's lots more to do. A walk along the boardwalk in the Lower Geyser Basin provides a close-up look at mud pots and other geo-thermal wonders. At the Grand Canyon of the Yellowstone, visitors stroll out to the scenic overlooks to soak in the beauty of Yellowstone's spectacular canyon. Lamar Valley is another popular spot. From the scenic drive, people might spot bison, bears, wolves, and other wildlife. And don't miss the park's many waterfalls.

Bison in Yellowstone National Park

Boat ride on Jenny Lake

★ **Grand Teton National Park:** Besides gaping at the magnificent mountains, many visitors take a boat ride across Jenny Lake to enjoy the view at Inspiration Point and hike through Cascade Canyon. Keep an eye out for moose and other wildlife!

★ **Colter Bay Indian Arts Museum:** This museum features an impressive collection of Native American crafts and artifacts.

★ **Snow King Resort:** Skiers and snowboarders hit the slopes at this resort, which is only a few blocks from town.

★ **National Elk Refuge:** In winter, you can take a sleigh ride among the nation's largest elk herd, just outside of town.

Jackson has only 9,000 residents but hosts more than 3 million tourists each year!

BUFFALO BILL CODY: FRONTIERSMAN AND SHOWMAN

William "Buffalo Bill" Cody (1846–1917) first arrived in Wyoming in 1858. Cody spent many years moving throughout the West as a scout, bison hunter, and frontiersman. In the 1890s, he helped to found the town of Cody. He gained worldwide fame by bringing the Wild West to audiences in the United States and Europe. His Buffalo Bill's Wild West show (1883–1913) was a rousing spectacle of cowboys, Indians, trick shooters, and other acts.

Want to know more? See www.pbs.org/weta/thewest/people/a_c/cody.htm

Cody

★ **Buffalo Bill Historical Center:** Here you can learn about the Wild West and the extraordinary life of Buffalo Bill Cody.

Buffalo Bill Historical Center

Mineral formations at Hot Springs State Park

Thermopolis

★ **Hot Springs State Park:** Take a dip in the soothing hot springs.

Wind River Indian Reservation

★ **Shoshone Tribal Cultural Center:** Take a tour of historical Fort Washakie to learn about Chief Washakie, Sacagawea, and Shoshone culture.

South Pass City

★ **South Pass City State Historic Site:** This site, the primary place where Oregon Trail travelers crossed the Continental Divide, features historic buildings from the 1867 gold rush.

NORTHEAST

THINGS TO DO: Go hiking, explore historic trails, and see a famous hideout.

Barnum

★ **Hole-in-the-Wall:** A scenic drive winds through the Hole-in-the-Wall Country, where Butch Cassidy and other outlaws hid from the law. For the adventurous, there's a 2.5-mile (4 km) hike over rugged terrain to the gap in the mountains.

Hulett

★ **Devils Tower National Monument:** A 1.3-mile (2 km) hike skirts the base of the tower. On the trail, keep an eye peeled for prairie dogs and other wildlife. Experienced rock climbers sometimes make their way up the tower cliffs.

Horseback riding near Devils Tower National Monument

Sheridan

★ **Don King's Western Museum:** Here you can see fancy Western saddles and memorabilia of the Wild West.

Story

★ **Fort Phil Kearny State Historic Site:** At this site, you can learn about the Indian Wars on the plains and life on the Bozeman Trail.

MINI-BIO

BUTCH CASSIDY: OUTLAW

Butch Cassidy was the assumed name of Robert LeRoy Parker (1866–1908?). Cassidy became a notorious train and bank robber in Wyoming and other Western states. His Wild Bunch gang hid out in the wilderness close to Cassidy's ranch near Dubois. According to one account, he was killed in a 1908 shoot-out following a robbery in Bolivia. Some friends and family members claimed to have seen Cassidy years later. The mystery remains.

 Want to know more? See www. wyomingtalesandtrails.com/butch.html

SOUTHEAST

THINGS TO DO: Watch a rodeo, take in some regional art, and count the names on Independence Rock.

Cheyenne

★ **Cheyenne Frontier Days:** Since 1897, this has been the world's largest outdoor rodeo and Western celebration.

★ **Big Boots:** Local artists made a bunch of 8-foot-tall (2.4 m) cowboy boots that are now scattered around town. They depict the history of Cheyenne and Wyoming.

A boot at the Union Pacific Railroad Depot

MINI-BIO

BRANDIE HALLS: BARREL RACER

Brandie Halls (1970–) is a barrel racer on the professional rodeo tour. Born in Torrington, she began barrel racing at an early age. Her mother had competed in barrel racing, and her father rode saddle broncs. Halls trains horses for competitions on her ranch near Carpenter. She travels to compete in rodeos throughout Wyoming and other Western states.

❓ **Want to know more?** See www.teamroper.com/Pro/RockyMountainRoper/Default.asp?Action=View&SubAction=EdArticle&ID=134

FAQ

Q8 HOW DID LARAMIE GET ITS NAME?

A8 Jacques LaRamie was one of the first white men who came to Wyoming to trap beavers and other animals. Not much is known about LaRamie but his name lives on in a river, a mountain range, a peak, a section of plains, a county, and a city in Wyoming.

Fort Laramie

★ **Fort Laramie National Historic Site:** The audio program that accompanies this tour has dramatic readings from diaries and journals of people who lived at the fort.

Laramie

★ **University of Wyoming:** The university includes excellent art and geology museums, and its American Heritage Center is one of the largest university archives in the United States.

★ **Wyoming Territorial Prison State Historic Site:** This site once housed the first territorial prison in Wyoming, the only prison where Butch Cassidy did time.

An exhibit at Wyoming Territorial Prison Historic Site

Guernsey

★ **Oregon Trail Ruts State Historic Site:** This site features well-preserved ruts made by wagons struggling up a steep hill. Some of the ruts are more than 5 feet (1.5 m) deep!

Encampment

★ **Grand Encampment Museum:** This museum is filled with artifacts from the mining and timber industries of the nearby Sierra Madre Mountains.

Casper

★ **National Historic Trails Interpretive Center:** Here you can learn about life on the pioneer trails.

★ **Nicolaysen Art Museum & Discovery Center:** Check out the exhibits of regional art at this museum. Be sure to see the tower clock in the lobby!

Alcova

★ **Independence Rock State Historic Site:** Thousands of pioneers who traveled west on the Oregon Trail wrote or scratched their names on a large chunk of granite.

SOUTHWEST

THINGS TO DO: See the fossil of an ancient crocodile, climb a huge sand dune, or learn about Wyoming's early fur trappers.

Kemmerer

★ **Fossil Butte National Monument:** Here you can check out fossils that are more than 50 million years old. You'll see ancient plants, fish, insects, birds, and even a crocodile that lived in this area when it was under the sea. You'll also catch a glimpse of living wildlife.

Rock Springs

★ **Killpecker Sand Dunes:** The largest sand dune system in the United States, this is part of the Red Desert.

Flaming Gorge National Recreation Area

Exploring at Fossil Butte National Monument

Green River

★ **Flaming Gorge National Recreation Area:** Here you can cast your line in the lake to try to catch trout, lake salmon, and bass.

Lyman

★ **Fort Bridger State Museum and Historic Site:** The historic buildings and museum exhibits here give a feel for the life of Wyoming's early fur trappers.

WRITING PROJECTS

Check out these ideas for creating a campaign brochure and writing you-are-there narratives. Or research the lives of famous people from Wyoming.

118

ART PROJECTS

You can illustrate the state song, create a dazzling PowerPoint presentation, or learn about the state quarter and design your own.

119

TIMELINE

What happened when? This timeline highlights important events in the state's history—and shows what was happening throughout the United States at the same time.

122

GLOSSARY

Remember the Words to Know from the chapters in this book? They're all collected here.

125

FAST FACTS

Use this section to find fascinating facts about state symbols, land area and population statistics, weather, sports teams, and much more.

126

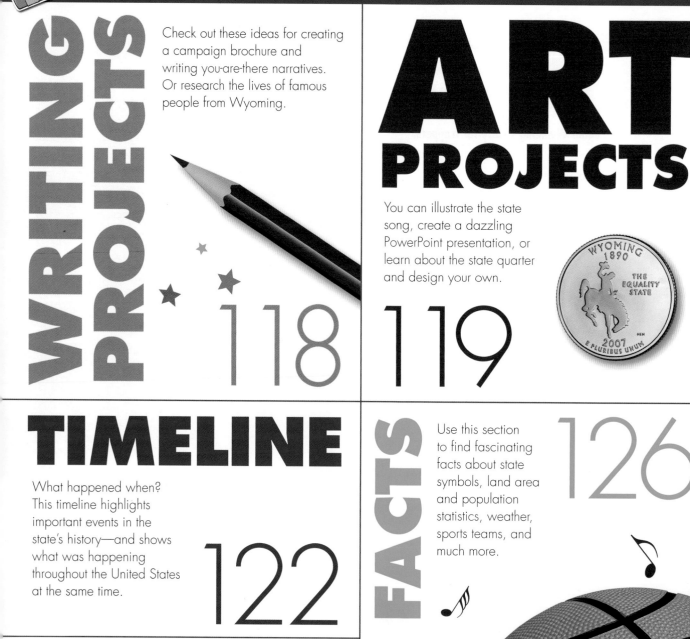

SCIENCE, TECHNOLOGY, & MATH PROJECTS

Make weather maps, graph population statistics, and research endangered species that live in the state.

120

PRIMARY VS. SECONDARY SOURCES

121

So what are primary and secondary sources? And what's the diff? This section explains all that and where you can find them.

BIOGRAPHICAL DICTIONARY

133

This at-a-glance guide highlights some of the state's most important and influential people. Visit this section and read about their contributions to the state, the country, and the world.

RESOURCES

Books, Web sites, DVDs, and more. Take a look at these additional sources for information about the state.

137

WRITING PROJECTS

★ ★ ★

Write a Memoir, Journal, or Editorial for Your School Newspaper!

Picture Yourself . . .

★ Building a tipi with the Crow people. These temporary structures were important for Crows and other Plains Indians, who moved their camps when following bison herds. Describe the process of building a tipi. What supplies or tools do you need?

SEE: Chapter Two, page 30.

GO TO: http://education.boisestate. edu/compass/Idahohistory/Chapter%203/ Mod2Ch3kids.htm

★ As a mountain man in Wyoming. What gear would you carry? What kinds of animals would you hunt? Describe the challenges you'd face each day.

SEE: Chapter Three, page 42.

GO TO: www.xmission.com/~drudy/

Create an Election Brochure or Web Site!

Run for office! Throughout this book, you've read about some of the issues that concern Wyoming today. As a candidate for governor of Wyoming, create a campaign brochure or Web site.

★ Explain how you meet the qualifications to be governor of Wyoming.

★ Talk about the three or four major issues you'll focus on if you're elected.

★ Remember, you'll be responsible for Wyoming's budget. How would you spend the taxpayers' money?

SEE: Chapter Seven, pages 90–91.

GO TO: Wyoming's Government Web site at http://wyoming.gov. You might also want to read some local newspapers. Try these:

Casper Star Tribune at www.casperstartribune. com

Wyoming Tribune Eagle at www.wyomingnews. com

Create an interview script with a famous person from Wyoming!

★ Research various Wyomingites, such as John Colter, Esther Morris, Washakie, Nellie Tayloe Ross, Liz Byrd, Mary O'Hara, Jackson Pollock, and Red Cloud.

★ Based on your research, pick one person you would most like to talk with.

★ Write a script of the interview. What questions would you ask? How would this person answer? Create a question-and-answer format. You may want to supplement this writing project with a voice-recording dramatization of the interview.

SEE: Chapters Three, Four, Five, and Six, pages 40, 55, 57, 67, 78, 83, and 84, and the Biographical Dictionary, pages 133–136.

ART PROJECTS

★ ★ ★

Create a PowerPoint Presentation or Visitors' Guide

Welcome to Wyoming!

Wyoming's a great place to visit and to live! From its natural beauty to its historical sites, there's plenty to see and do. In your PowerPoint presentation or brochure, highlight 10 to 15 of Wyoming's fascinating landmarks. Be sure to include:

★ a map of the state showing where these sites are located

★ photos, illustrations, Web links, natural history facts, geographic stats, climate and weather, plants and wildlife, and recent discoveries

SEE: Chapter Nine, pages 108–115, and Fast Facts, pages 126–127.

GO TO: The official tourism Web site for Wyoming at www.wyomingtourism.org. Download and print maps, photos, and vacation ideas for tourists.

Illustrate the Lyrics to the Wyoming State Song

("Wyoming")

Use markers, paints, photos, collages, colored pencils, or computer graphics to illustrate the lyrics to "Wyoming." Turn your illustrations into a picture book, or scan them into PowerPoint and add music.

SEE: The lyrics to "Wyoming" on page 128.

GO TO: Wyoming's government Web site at http://wyoming.gov to find out more about the origin of the state song.

State Quarter Project

From 1999 to 2008, the U.S. Mint introduced new quarters commemorating each of the 50 states in the order that they were admitted to the Union. Each state's quarter features a unique design on its back, or reverse.

GO TO: www.usmint.gov/kids and find out what's featured on the back of the Wyoming quarter.

★ Research the significance of the image. Who designed the quarter? Who chose the final design?

★ Design your own Wyoming quarter. What images would you choose for the reverse?

★ Make a poster showing the Wyoming quarter and label each image.

SCIENCE, TECHNOLOGY, & MATH PROJECTS

★ ★ ★

Graph Population Statistics!

★ Compare population statistics (such as ethnic background, birth, death, and literacy rates) in Wyoming counties or major cities. In your graph or chart, look at population density and write sentences describing what the population statistics show; graph one set of population statistics and write a paragraph explaining what the graphs reveal.

SEE: Chapter Six, pages 77–80.

GO TO: The official Web site for the U.S. Census Bureau at www.census.gov and at http://quickfacts.census.gov/qfd/states/56000.html to find out more about population statistics, how they work, and what the statistics are for Wyoming.

Create a Weather Map of Wyoming!

Use your knowledge of Wyoming's geography to research and identify conditions that result in specific weather events. What is it about the geography of Wyoming that makes it vulnerable to things like blizzards? Create a weather map or poster that shows the weather patterns over the state. Include a caption explaining the technology used to measure weather phenomena, and provide data.

SEE: Chapter One, pages 18–19.

GO TO: The National Oceanic and Atmospheric Administration's National Weather Service Web site at www.weather.gov for weather maps and forecasts for Wyoming.

Black-footed ferret

Track Endangered Species

Using your knowledge of Wyoming's wildlife, research which animals and plants are endangered or threatened.

★ Find out what the state is doing to protect these species.

★ Chart known populations of the animals and plants, and report on changes in certain geographic areas.

SEE: Chapter One, page 23.

GO TO: Web sites such as http://ecos.fws.gov/tess_public/StateListingAndOccurrence.do?state=WY for lists of endangered species in Wyoming.

PRIMARY VS. SECONDARY SOURCES

★ ★ ★

What's the Diff?

Your teacher may require at least one or two primary sources and one or two secondary sources for your assignment. So, what's the difference between the two?

★ **Primary sources are original.** You are reading the actual words of someone's diary, journal, letter, autobiography, or interview. Primary sources can also be photographs, maps, prints, cartoons, news/film footage, posters, first-person newspaper articles, drawings, musical scores, and recordings. By the way, when you conduct a survey, interview someone, shoot a video, or take photographs to include in a project, you are creating primary sources!

★ **Secondary sources are what you find in encyclopedias, textbooks, articles, biographies, and almanacs.** These are written by a person or group of people who tell about something that happened to someone else. Secondary sources also recount what another person said or did. This book is an example of a secondary source.

Now that you know what primary sources are—where can you find them?

★ **Your school or local library:** Check the library catalog for collections of original writings, government documents, musical scores, and so on. Some of this material may be stored on microfilm. The Library of Congress Web site (www.loc.gov) is an excellent online resource for primary source materials.

★ **Historical societies:** These organizations keep historical documents, photographs, and other materials. Staff members can help you find what you are looking for. History museums are also great places to see primary sources firsthand.

★ **The Internet:** There are lots of sites that have primary sources you can download and use in a project or assignment.

TIMELINE

★ ★ ★

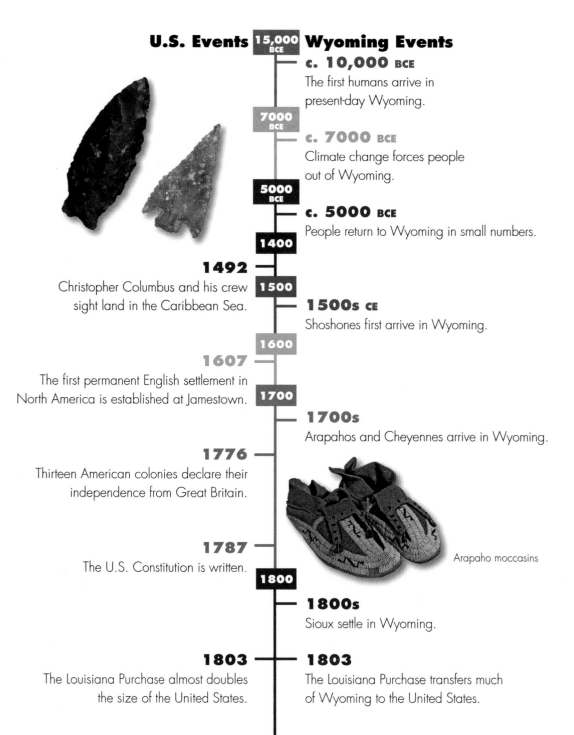

U.S. Events		Wyoming Events
	15,000 BCE	
		c. 10,000 BCE The first humans arrive in present-day Wyoming.
	7000 BCE	
		c. 7000 BCE Climate change forces people out of Wyoming.
	5000 BCE	
		c. 5000 BCE People return to Wyoming in small numbers.
	1400	
1492 Christopher Columbus and his crew sight land in the Caribbean Sea.	**1500**	
		1500s CE Shoshones first arrive in Wyoming.
	1600	
1607 The first permanent English settlement in North America is established at Jamestown.	**1700**	
		1700s Arapahos and Cheyennes arrive in Wyoming.
1776 Thirteen American colonies declare their independence from Great Britain.		
1787 The U.S. Constitution is written.	**1800**	Arapaho moccasins
		1800s Sioux settle in Wyoming.
1803 The Louisiana Purchase almost doubles the size of the United States.		**1803** The Louisiana Purchase transfers much of Wyoming to the United States.

7000 BCE

c. 7000 BCE
Climate change forces people out of Wyoming.

5000 BCE

c. 5000 BCE
People return to Wyoming in small numbers.

1400

1492
Christopher Columbus and his crew sight land in the Caribbean Sea.

1500

1500s CE
Shoshones first arrive in Wyoming.

1600

1607
The first permanent English settlement in North America is established at Jamestown.

1700

1700s
Arapahos and Cheyennes arrive in Wyoming.

1776
Thirteen American colonies declare their independence from Great Britain.

Arapaho moccasins

1787
The U.S. Constitution is written.

1800

1800s
Sioux settle in Wyoming.

1803
The Louisiana Purchase almost doubles the size of the United States.

1803
The Louisiana Purchase transfers much of Wyoming to the United States.

U.S. Events

Wyoming Events

1806
John Colter arrives in Wyoming.

1812-15
The United States and Great Britain fight the War of 1812.

1820s
Mountain men come to Wyoming to trap for furs.

1830
The Indian Removal Act forces eastern Native American groups to relocate west of the Mississippi River.

1840s
The era of the mountain men ends.

1850
Fifty-five thousand people travel across Wyoming on the Oregon Trail.

Oregon Trail

1860
Pony Express riders cross Wyoming.

1861-65
The American Civil War is fought between the Northern Union and the Southern Confederacy; it ends with the surrender of the Confederate army, led by General Robert E. Lee.

1861
Wyoming becomes part of the Dakota Territory.

1867
The Union Pacific Railroad is laid in Wyoming.

1869
Wyoming is organized as a territory.

1877
The U.S. Army drives the remaining Sioux out of Wyoming.

1886
Apache leader Geronimo surrenders to the U.S. Army, ending the last major Native American rebellion against the expansion of the United States into the West.

1890
Wyoming becomes the 44th state.

1898
The United States gains control of Cuba, Puerto Rico, the Philippines, and Guam after defeating Spain in the Spanish-American War.

1900

1903
A coal mine accident in Hanna claims the lives of 169 men.

U.S. Events

1917–18
The United States engages in World War I.

1920
The Nineteenth Amendment to the U.S. Constitution grants women the right to vote.

1929
The stock market crashes, plunging the United States more deeply into the Great Depression.

1941–45
The United States engages in World War II.

1951–53
The United States engages in the Korean War.

1954
The U.S. Supreme Court prohibits segregation of public schools in the *Brown v. Board of Education* ruling.

1964–73
The United States engages in the Vietnam War.

1991
The United States and other nations engage in the brief Persian Gulf War against Iraq.

2000

2001
Terrorists attack the United States on September 11.

2008
The United States elects its first African American president, Barack Obama.

Wyoming Events

1925
Nellie Tayloe Ross becomes the nation's first female governor.

1950s
Uranium deposits are discovered in the Powder River, Shirley, and Wind River basins.

1957
The legislature passes the Wyoming Civil Rights Act.

1970s
Wyoming's population soars as the oil industry booms.

1988
Fires destroy large swaths of Yellowstone National Park.

2000s
Demand for Wyoming's coal supply grows.

Nellie Tayloe Ross

Oil well

GLOSSARY

★ ★ ★

archaeologists people who study the remains of past human societies

coal bed methane a natural gas found in layers (beds) of coal

constitution a written document that contains all the governing principles of a state or country

dry goods clothing, cloth, and related goods

endangered at risk of becoming extinct

erosion the gradual wearing away of rock or soil by physical breakdown, chemical solution, or water

geologists scientists who study the history of Earth

geothermal relating to or produced by the heat of Earth's core

geysers springs that shoot steam and hot water from underground into the air

igneous formed by the hardening of melted rock

irrigation watering land by artificial means to promote plant growth

loincloth a strip of cloth or leather worn between the legs that passes over a belt or cord tied around the waist

magma melted rock that has not yet erupted

nomadic describing someone who moves from place to place and does not permanently settle in one location

nuclear weapons bombs or devices that use the energy created by splitting certain atoms (such as uranium) to create large explosions

Plains Indians nations of bison hunters who lived from the Mississippi River west to the Rockies and from Texas north to central Canada

radioactive giving off atomic particles, which can be dangerous to living things

receded pulled or moved back over time

sedimentary formed from clay, sand, and gravel that settled at the bottom of a body of water

segregated separated from others, according to race, class, ethnic group, religion, or other factors

suffrage the right to vote

surveyors people who measure land to set boundaries or mark building sites

threatened likely to become endangered in the foreseeable future

tributaries smaller rivers that flow into a larger river

union an organization formed by workers to try to improve working conditions and wages

FAST FACTS

★ ★ ★

State Symbols

State seal

Statehood date	July 10,1890; the 44th state
Origin of state name	From two words in the language of the Delaware people: *wama*, meaning "plains," and *maughwau*, meaning "large"
State capital	Cheyenne
State nickname	Equality State, Big Wyoming, Cowboy State
State motto	"Equal Rights"
State bird	Meadowlark
State flower	Indian paintbrush
State fish	Cutthroat trout
State mammal	Bison
State reptile	Horned toad
State dinosaur	Triceratops
State fossil	Knightia
State gemstone	Jade
State song	"Wyoming"
State tree	Plains cottonwood
State fair	Late August at Douglas

Geography

Total area; rank	97,814 square miles (253,337 sq km); 10th
Land; rank	97,100 square miles (251,488 sq km); 9th
Water; rank	713 square miles (1,847 sq km); 36th
Inland water; rank	713 square miles (1,847 sq km); 30th
Geographic center	Fremont, 58 miles (93 km) east-northeast of Lander
Latitude	41° N to 45° N
Longitude	104°3' W to 111°3' W
Highest point	Gannett Peak, 13,809 feet (4,209 m), in Fremont County
Lowest point	Belle Fourche River, 3,099 feet (945 m), in Crook County
Largest city	Cheyenne
Number of counties	23
Longest river	North Platte River

Population

Population; rank (2007 estimate)	522,830; 51st
Density (2007 estimate)	5 persons per square mile (2 per sq km)
Population distribution (2000 census)	65% urban, 35% rural
Race (2007 estimate)	White persons: 94.1%*
	American Indian and Alaska Native persons: 2.5%*
	Black persons: 1.2%*
	Asian persons: 0.7%*
	Native Hawaiian and Other Pacific Islanders: 0.1%*
	Persons reporting two or more races: 1.4%
	Persons of Hispanic or Latino origin: 7.4%†
	White persons not Hispanic: 87.3%

* Includes persons reporting only one race.
† Hispanics may be of any race, so they are also included in applicable race categories.

Weather

Record high temperature	115°F (46°C) at Basin on August 8, 1983
Record low temperature	−66°F (−54°C) near Moran on February 9, 1933
Average July temperature	71°F (22°C)
Average January temperature	20°F (−7°C)
Average yearly precipitation	13 inches (33 cm)

State flag

STATE SONG

★ ★ ★

"Wyoming"

"Wyoming," with words by Charles E. Winter and music by George E. Knapp, was adopted as the official state song on February 15, 1955.

In the far and mighty West,
Where the crimson sun seeks rest,
There's a growing splendid state that lies above
On the breast of this great land;
Where the massive Rockies stand,
There's Wyoming young and strong, the State I love!

Chorus:
Wyoming! Wyoming! Land of the sunlight clear!
Wyoming, Wyoming! Land that we hold so dear!
Wyoming, Wyoming! Precious art thou and thine!
Wyoming, Wyoming! Beloved State of mine!

In thy flowers wild and sweet,
Colors rare and perfumes meet;
There's the columbine so pure, the daisy too,
Wild the rose and red it springs,
White the button and its rings,
Thou art loyal for they're red and white and blue.

(Chorus)

Where thy peaks with crowned head,
Rising till the sky they wed,
Sit like snow queens ruling wood and stream and
    plain;
'Neath thy granite bases deep,
'Neath thy bosom's broadened sweep,
Lie the riches that have gained and brought thee fame.

(Chorus)

Other treasures thou dost hold,
Men and women thou dost mould;
True and earnest are the lives that thou dost raise;
Strength thy children thou dost teach,
Nature's truth thou givest to each,
Free and noble are thy workings and thy ways.

(Chorus)

In the nation's banner free
There's one star that has for me
A radiance pure and splendor like the sun;
Mine it is, Wyoming's star,
Home it leads me, near or far;
O Wyoming! All my heart and love you've won!

(Chorus)

NATURAL AREAS AND HISTORIC SITES

★　★　★

National Parks

Grand Teton National Park, located in northwestern Wyoming, is home to elk, moose, deer, and more than 300 species of birds, among other animals.

Yellowstone National Park, the oldest national park in the nation, has many geysers, hot springs, and other geothermal features.

National Recreation Areas

Bighorn Canyon National Recreation Area is filled with lakes, rivers, and a magnificent canyon. It was created following the construction of the Yellowtail Dam.

Flaming Gorge National Recreation Area, which lies on the Utah–Wyoming border, features brightly colored cliffs surrounding Flaming Gorge Lake.

National Monuments

Devils Tower National Monument is a stunning rock formation that rises more than 1,200 feet (370 m) above the surrounding terrain. It was the nation's first national monument.

Fossil Butte National Monument is a 50-million-year-old lake bed that preserves fossils that span more than 2 million years.

Memorial Parkway

John D. Rockefeller Jr. Memorial Parkway connects Grand Teton and Yellowstone national parks.

National Historic Site

Fort Laramie National Historic Site was both a military post and a trading post.

National Historic Trails

Wyoming boasts four national historic trails: the *California National Historic Trail*; the *Mormon Pioneer National Historic Trail*; the *Nez Perce National Historic Trail*; the *Oregon National Historic Trail*, and the *Pony Express National Historic Trail*.

National Forests

Wyoming is home to seven national forests: *Ashley National Forest*, *Bighorn National Forest*, *Black Hills National Forest*, *Bridger-Teton National Forest*, *Medicine Bow-Routt National Forest*, *Shoshone National Forest*, and *Caribou-Targhee National Forest*.

State Parks

Wyoming's state park system maintains 25 state parks and historic sites, including *Buffalo Bill State Park*, which commemorates the life of William "Buffalo Bill" Cody; and *Hot Springs State Park*, Wyoming's first state park.

SPORTS TEAMS

NCAA Teams (Division I)

University of Wyoming *Cowboys*

The Wyoming Cowboys basketball team takes on the Arizona Wildcats.

CULTURAL INSTITUTIONS

★ ★ ★

Libraries

The *William Robertson Coe Library* at the University of Wyoming at Laramie is the state's largest library.

The *Wyoming State Library of Wyoming* (Cheyenne), the state's second-largest library, houses a valuable collection of law literature. This library was established in 1871 as the Wyoming Territorial Library.

Museums

The *University of Wyoming Art Museum* (Laramie) has an extensive collection of European, American, and Asian paintings, sculptures, photographs, and prints.

The *National Museum of Wildlife Art* (Jackson Hole) has an impressive collection of paintings, sculptures, and other artworks dating from 2000 BCE to the present.

Wyoming State Museum (Cheyenne) contains fine exhibits about pioneer days and Native American heritage.

Cheyenne Frontier Days Old West Museum features collections about pioneer life and Native American history.

Buffalo Bill Historical Center (Cody) commemorates the life and preserves the belongings of the famous hunter and Wild West showman.

The *University of Wyoming Geological Museum* (Laramie) displays fine collections on natural history including fossils, minerals, and rocks as well as exhibits about prehistoric times.

Universities and Colleges

In 2006, Wyoming had nine public institutions and one private institution of higher learning.

ANNUAL EVENTS

January–March

Cutter races near Afton, Big Piney, Jackson, Pinedale, and Saratoga (February)

Glass Art Celebration in Cheyenne (February)

Sagebrush Cowboy Gathering in Sheridan (February)

Waterfall Ice Festival in Cody (February)

Wyoming State Winter Fair in Lander (early March)

April–June

Cowboy Songs and Range Ballads in Cody (April)

Woodchoppers Jamboree in Encampment (mid-June)

Chugwater Chili Cook-off (June)

Plains Indian Powwow in Cody (June)

July–September

Pioneer Days in Lander (early July)

Central Wyoming Fair in Casper (mid-July)

Jubilee Days in Laramie (July)

Indian Sun Dances in Ethete and Fort Washakie (July)

Cheyenne Frontier Days (July)

Cody Stampede Rodeo (July)

Green River Rendezvous near Pinedale (July)

Sheridan Rodeo (July)

Indian Pageant in Thermopolis (early August)

Wyoming State Fair in Douglas (late August)

Evanston Cowboy Days (Labor Day)

Fort Bridger Rendezvous (Labor Day)

Jackson Hole Fall Arts Festival in Jackson Hole (mid-September and early October)

October–December

Wyoming Arts Alliance Showcase in Gillette (October)

Native American Artifacts Show in Gillette (November)

Feast of St. Andrew Ceilidh in Jackson (November)

Christmas Stroll in Sheridan (December)

BIOGRAPHICAL DICTIONARY

James Beckwourth (1800?–1866) was an African American mountain man, soldier, and explorer. He led a remarkable life, trapping furs in Wyoming, living with the Blackfoot and Crow peoples, and scouting for the U.S. Army.

Bud Boller (1928–) is an award-winning sculptor who lives on the Wind River Indian Reservation.

Jim Bridger See page 43.

Jerry Buss (1934–) is the owner of the Los Angeles Lakers, a professional basketball team. This Kemmerer native graduated from the University of Wyoming.

Liz Byrd See page 78.

Calamity Jane (1852?–1903) was born Martha Jane Cannary, but was better known by her nickname. She dressed as a man and worked as a scout for the U.S. Army in Wyoming in the 1860s and early 1870s.

Jerry Buss

Calamity Jane

Kit Carson (1809–1868) was a scout and frontiersman. He trapped beaver in Wyoming in the 1830s and became one of the legendary figures of the frontier.

Butch Cassidy See page 112.

Dick Cheney See page 94.

John Clymer (1907–1989) was an artist whose paintings of the Western frontier are known for their historical accuracy. He traveled throughout Wyoming to research his subjects and moved to Teton Village in 1980.

Buffalo Bill Cody See page 111.

John Colter See page 40.

June Etta Downey (1875–1932) was a prominent psychologist and educator. This Laramie native was a professor of psychology at the University of Wyoming.

Gretel Ehrlich (1946–) writes fiction, nonfiction, and essays. Works based on her experiences living in Wyoming include *The Solace of Open Spaces, A Match to the Heart,* and *Heart Mountain.*

Thomas Fitzpatrick See page 49.

Harrison Ford (1942–) is an actor known for roles in the Star Wars and Indiana Jones movie series. He owns an 800-acre (324 ha) ranch near Jackson.

Matthew Fox (1966–) is an actor known for his roles in the TV series *Party of Five* and *Lost.* He was raised on his family's horse ranch in Crowheart.

David Freudenthal See page 91.

Rulon Gardner (1971–) of Afton won the gold medal in Greco-Roman wrestling at the 2000 Summer Olympics and the bronze medal in 2004.

Curt Gowdy (1919–2006) was a leading sportscaster from the 1950s through the 1980s. This Green River native announced 16 World Series, eight Super Bowls, and seven Olympic Games.

Matthew Fox

Gretel Ehrlich

Brandie Halls See page 113.

Leonard Hobbs (1896–1977) was an aeronautical engineer and test pilot. This Carbon County native gained fame for designing the Pratt & Whitney J57, the world's first turbojet engine.

Tom Horn (1860–1903) was a detective for the Pinkerton Detective Agency. He purportedly killed about two dozen alleged rustlers. He was executed by hanging for a murder he may not have committed.

David Jackson (1788–1837) was a mountain man and fur trapper. Jackson Hole is named after him.

Isabel Jewell (1907–1972) was an actress who starred in *Gone with the Wind, High Sierra, Northwest Passage,* and *Lost Horizon.* Born in Shoshoni, she has a star on Hollywood's Walk of Fame.

Don King (1923–2007) was a famous saddle maker who was born in Douglas. Today, his trophy saddles are awarded at rodeos.

Chris LeDoux (1948–2005) was a professional rodeo cowboy and musician. He won the world bareback riding championship in 1976. He retired four years later, buying a ranch near Kaycee. He released his first major-label recording in 1991.

Patricia MacLachlan (1938–) is a children's book author. This Cheyenne native is best known for her novel *Sarah, Plain and Tall*.

Jason Miller See page 85.

Thomas Moran (1837–1926) was a painter whose works depict Western landscapes. His paintings of northeastern Wyoming motivated Congress to create Yellowstone National Park. Mount Moran in the Grand Tetons range is named after him.

Esther H. Morris See page 55.

Jill Morrison See page 23.

Danelle Moyte See page 79.

Bill Nye (1850–1896) was a journalist who wrote humorous articles. He founded and edited the *Laramie Boomerang*, a daily newspaper named after his mule. The newspaper is still in operation.

Patricia MacLachlan

Mary O'Hara (1885–1980) wrote popular novels including *My Friend Flicka*, which is about a boy and his horse. She and her husband operated Remount Ranch, a summer camp for boys in Laramie County.

J. C. Penney See page 105.

Jackson Pollock See page 84.

Annie Proulx (1935–) was the first woman to win the PEN/Faulkner Award for fiction (1993). She moved to Wyoming in 1995, and all of the stories in her collection *Close Range: Wyoming Stories* are set in the rural areas of the state.

Red Cloud (1822–1909) was a Sioux leader. He won a two-year conflict (1866–1868) with the U.S. Army over control of the Powder River Basin in Wyoming, and the U.S. government agreed to abandon its forts along the Bozeman Trail.

Teno Roncalio See page 71.

Nellie Tayloe Ross See page 67.

Red Cloud

Alan K. Simpson (1931–) represented Wyoming in the U.S. Senate for three terms (1979–1997). This Republican leader was known for his wit and folksy style.

Jedediah Smith (1799–1831?) was a fur trapper, mountain man, and explorer in Wyoming and elsewhere in the West.

Gerry Spence (1929–) is a successful author and lawyer who has represented many high-profile clients. He was born in Laramie and is now based in Jackson.

Elinore Pruitt Stewart (1876–1933) wrote about her experiences living on an isolated ranch near Burntfork. Her letters to a friend were published in the *Atlantic Monthly* and collected in *Letters of a Woman Homesteader* and *Letters on an Elk Hunt.*

William Sublette (1799–1845) was an early mountain man and pioneer. Along with Jedediah Smith and David Jackson, he operated a fur-trapping business in Wyoming.

Sundance Kid

Sundance Kid (1867–1908?) was the assumed name of outlaw Harry Longabaugh. A member of Butch Cassidy's Wild Bunch gang, he robbed trains and banks. The gang hid out in Wyoming.

Willis Van Devanter See page 93.

Francis E. Warren See page 90.

Washakie See page 57.

Owen Wister (1860–1938) was a writer who specialized in Western fiction. He spent several summers traveling in Wyoming, which provided the setting for his best-known work, *The Virginian*. It is considered to be the first Western novel.

Owen Wister

RESOURCES

★ ★ ★

BOOKS

Nonfiction

Cody, William F. *The Adventures of Buffalo Bill*. New York: Cosimo Classics, 2005.

Ditchfield, Christin. *The Arapaho*. New York: Children's Press, 2005.

Ditchfield, Christin. *The Shoshone*. New York: Children's Press, 2005.

Landau, Elaine. *The Transcontinental Railroad*. New York: Franklin Watts, 2005.

Monroe, Judy. *Chief Red Cloud: 1822–1909*. Mankato, Minn.: Blue Earth, 2003.

Palmer, Rosemary G. *Jim Bridger: Trapper, Trader, and Guide*. Mankato, Minn.: Compass Point, 2007.

Petersen, David. *Yellowstone National Park*. New York: Children's Press, 2001.

Stewart, Elinore Pruitt. *Letters of a Woman Homesteader*. Lincoln, Neb.: Bison, 1990.

Warren, Louis S. *Buffalo Bill's America: William Cody and the Wild West Show*. New York: Knopf, 2005.

Fiction

Ehrlich, Gretel. *A Blizzard Year*. New York: Hyperion, 1999.

Gagliano, Eugene. *Secret of the Black Widow*. Shippensburg, Penn.: White Mane, 2002.

Naylor, Phyllis Reynolds. *Walker's Crossing*. New York: Atheneum, 1999.

O'Hara, Mary. *Green Grass of Wyoming*. HarperCollins, 1988.

O'Hara, Mary. *My Friend Flicka*. New York: HarperFestival, 2003.

Ryan, Pam Muñoz. *Paint the Wind*. New York: Scholastic, 2007.

Schaefer, Jack. *Shane*. Boston: Houghton Mifflin, 2001.

Skurzynski, Gloria, and Alane Ferguson. *Wolf Stalker*. Washington, D.C.: National Geographic Society, 1997.

Wister, Owen. *The Virginian*. New York: Pocket Books, 2002.

DVDs

American Experience: Buffalo Bill. PBS, 2008.
Chiefs. LifeSize, 2006.
Investigating History: Butch Cassidy & the Sundance Kid. A&E Home Video, 2005.
Miracle at Sage Creek. Universal, 2005.

WEB SITES AND ORGANIZATIONS

American Experience: Buffalo Bill
www.pbs.org/wgbh/amex/cody
Learn about the legendary frontiersman and showman.

American Experience: Transcontinental Railroad
www.pbs.org/wgbh/amex/tcrr
Find out about the building of the Union Pacific and Central Pacific railroads.

The Oregon Trail
www.pbs.org/weta/thewest/places/trails_ter/oregon.htm
Get information about the Oregon Trail's people, historic sites, and timeline.

Shoshone Tribe
www.easternshoshone.net
Find out more about Wyoming's largest Native American nation.

State of Wyoming
http://wyoming.gov
This site offers information about how the state government works.

Wyoming Tourism
www.wyomingtourism.org
Research fun places to visit in Wyoming.

Yellowstone National Park
www.nps.gov/yell
Explore the world's first national park.

INDEX

★ ★ ★

AUTHOR'S TIPS AND SOURCE NOTES

★ ★ ★

When researching this book, I found T. A. Larson's *Wyoming: A Bicentennial History* to be a great resource. It provided in-depth information on Wyoming's history from its territorial days until the mid-1970s. To learn about Wyoming's Indians, I used books on Native Americans in my personal library and read books on the Shoshone, Arapaho, Crow, and Cheyenne nations. Other books that were helpful include Francis Parkman's *The Oregon Trail*, Stephen Ambrose's *Nothing Like It in the World: The Men Who Built the Transcontinental Railroad, 1863–1869,* and John D. McDermott's *A Guide to the Indian Wars of the West*.

There were also many great resources online. I found information on Buffalo Bill, the Oregon Trail, and the transcontinental railroad at www.pbs.org. The official State of Wyoming's site (http://wyoming.gov) provided much information on the state government and other topics.

Photographs © 2010: Alamy Images: 87 right, 88, 111 top right (John Elk III), 50 bottom (Stephen Finn), 98, 99 left (GlowImages), 115 right (Zach Holmes), 29 (Interfoto Pressebildagentur), 113 bottom (Andre Jenny), 37 top right, 43 top, 47 (North Wind Picture Archives); American Heritage Center, University of Wyoming: 36 bottom, 40 top (Dave Paulley/Dave Miles Photography/Wyoming State Historical Society), 52, 54; American Museum of Natural History/North American Ethnographic Collection: 35, 122 bottom (50/1028AB), 4 top center, 25 bottom (50/2333); Courtesy of Ann Fuller: 23 left; AP Images: 113 top (Isaac Brekken), 75 right, 85 left (Andy Carpenean/Laramie Boomerang), 94 top (Ron Edmonds), 104 (Nati Harnik), 85 right (Jae C. Hong), 66, 90, 93; Art Resource, NY/Smithsonian American Art Museum, Washington, DC: 31; Bridgeman Art Library International Ltd., London/New York: 44, 123 top (Butler Institute of American Art, Youngstown, OH/Gift of Joseph G. Butler III, 1946), 36 top, 37 top left (Museum of Fine Arts, Boston/Gift of Martha C. Karolik for the M. and M. Karolik), 25 top right, 34, 40 bottom, 48, 56 (Private Collection/Peter Newark American Pictures), 43 bottom, 46 (Walters Art Museum, Baltimore); Colorado Historical Society/BPF Collection: 49 (Scan #10027099); Corbis Images: 5 top left, 58 (Bettmann), 112 right (Jonathan Blair), 24 top, 25 top left (Werner Forman), 51 top right, 61 (Gleason Studio), 65 top right, 68 (Jay Higgins), 76 (Wolfgang Kaehler), back cover, cover main (Kevin R. Morris), 94 bottom (Larry W. Smith), 74, 75 left (Swift/Vanuga Images), 64 bottom, 67, 124 top; Courtesy of Danelle Moyte-Fernandez: 79; Danita Delimont Stock Photography: 111 bottom (Sergio Pitamitz), 80 (Jamie & Judy Wild); Denver Public Library, Western History Collection: 55 (X-18554), 32 (X-32361); Getty Images: 59 (Geoff Brightling), 20 (Guy Crittenden), 24 bottom, 122 top (Jeff Foott), 134 bottom (Jesse Grant), 84 (Martha Holmes), 83 (Marc McAndrews), 99 right, 102 (Michael Medford), 13 (Eastcott Momatiuk), 5 top right, 65 bottom, 124 bottom (Joel Sartore), 18 (David Stubbs); iStockphoto: 116 bottom, 130 bottom (Geoffrey Black), 130 top (David Freund), 5 top center, 51 bottom, 123 bottom (Hannamaria Photography), 53 (Stefan Klein), 128 (Vladislav Lebedinski), 37 bottom (mikadx), 4 top left, 9 right, 19 (Maurice van der Velden); Kevin Moloney Photography: 82, 91 right, 91 left; Library of Congress: 136 bottom (Brain News Service), 136 top (DeYoung Photograph Studio, NYC), 57 (Rose & Hopkins), 135 bottom; Lonely Planet Images: 17 (John Elk III), 73 (Corinne Humphrey); National Geographic Image Collection: 115 left (Melissa Farlow), 26 (Charles R. Knight), 100 (Tomasz Tomaszewski); NEWSCOM: 133 top (Darryl Dennis/Icon SMI), 134 top (Susan Pollard/Contra Costa Times), 135 top (SHNS/Pittsburgh Arts & Lectures); Niebrugge Images/Ron Niebrugge: 8, 9 left; Photo Researchers, NY/Alan & Sandy Carey: 23 right, 120; PhotoEdit: 107 (David Frazier), 114 (Clayton Sharrard); Reuters/Adrees Latif: 130 center; Science Faction Images/Louie Psihoyos: 10; ShutterStock, Inc.: 22 (Ferenc Cegledi), 132 (Olivier Le Queinec), 121 (Monkey Business Images), 110 bottom (Bartosz Wardinski); Southern Methodist University, DeGolyer Library/JCPenney Archives Collection: 105; StockFood, Inc.: 81 bottom (Fotos mitgeschmack/GU), 4 bottom, 81 top (John Kelly/Food Image Source); The Granger Collection, New York: 4 top right, 33, 41, 50 top, 51 top left, 62, 63, 111 top left, 133 bottom; The Image Works: 5 bottom, 112 left (David Frazier), 110 top (Andre Jenny); U.S. Mint: 116 top, 119; Vector-Images.com: 4 center, 96, 97, 126, 127; VEER/Ron Watts: 15; Wyoming State Archives/Department of State Parks and Cultural Resources: 64 top, 65 top left (From the J.E. Stimson Collection), 69, 71 top, 71 bottom, 78, 86, 87 left; Wyoming State Museum, Department of State Parks and Cultural Resources: cover inset (ETHN-1958.18.4).

Maps by Map Hero, Inc.